SLEEPING AMONG SHEEP UNDER A STARRY SKY

Wallace Shawn

SLEEPING AMONG SHEEP UNDER A STARRY SKY

ESSAYS 1985-2021

Europa
editions

Europa Editions
8 Blackstock Mews
London N4 2BT
www.europaeditions.co.uk

First publication 2022 by Europa Editions

A catalogue record for this title is available from the British Library
ISBN 978-1-78770-363-6

Shawn, Wallace
Sleeping Among Sheep Under a Starry Sky

Art direction by Emanuele Ragnisco
instagram.com/emanueleragnisco

Cover design and illustration by Ginevra Rapisardi

Photo © Don J Usner

Prepress by Grafica Punto Print – Rome

Printed and bound in Great Britain by Clays Ltd, Elcograf S.p.A.

CONTENTS

With love, to Allen

SLEEPING AMONG SHEEP UNDER A STARRY SKY

Introduction

When I was a five-year-old child, I had the opportunity to play the part of a shepherd in a Christmas pageant on a wonderful stage with wonderfully painted scenery, and the magical, magically shifting lighting, representing the peaceful night outside of Bethlehem, where we slept among our sheep and then dimly awakened, made an impression on me that can't be easily explained.

In the next few years after the Christmas pageant, I received an education that perfectly suited the mood of its time and place—a lovely neighborhood in New York City in the 1950's, glowing with beautiful expectations. Fascism had been defeated, and our parents and their friends found no reason to doubt that the prosperity we enjoyed would inevitably expand—expand to embrace all human beings—while our teachers believed that the most significant challenge for each one of us was simply to discover what role in society best suited our particular inclinations. Poverty would end. Hunger would end. Our individual obligation was simply to figure out what we most enjoyed doing, because that would be the thing we would inevitably do best. Did we want to work in some fantastic industry, producing goods that would make daily life better and easier for the world's people? Or did we want to nourish their spirits by giving them paintings, stories, or wonderful concerts? The people in our neighborhood were simply not in the right frame of mind to take the hints provided by the recent murder of Jews, Roma, and homosexuals in Europe, not to mention by the history of slavery in the United States, not to mention by the siege of Carthage, the

Crusades, and what have you, that terrible dangers lurked within us.

In the 1960's I studied a bit more, and my education was of the kind that might have permitted me to try to become, perhaps, an international civil servant of some sort, or a diplomat, or even (who knows?) an intellectual of some description—but the mesmeric power of the magically shifting Christmas pageant lighting pulled me back towards the memory of the scene I'd been in. The uncanny lighting had enchanted me, and it turned out that in the end I never escaped from it. I considered escaping, I was tempted to escape, but I guess I never seriously tried to escape. It turned out that I devoted my life to writing plays, and I even became an actor as well, never again called upon to play a shepherd but frequently summoned to provide a voice for talking animals of every kind in cartoons intended for five-year-old children.

Well, there's only a very thin curtain between theatre and life, if I may use that metaphor. I mean, a lot of people have raised questions, for example, about whether music is "about" anything, and various people have puzzled in one way or another over the degree to which a poem is "about" something or just "is" something, but almost no one has ever tried to say that theatre is not about the world. And people involved with theatre can often be found brooding about their chosen subject matter. Aeschylus, Sophocles, and Euripides started the Western playwriting tradition by writing plays about politics. Someone recently told me about a great filmmaker who found it difficult to come to the set because it obliged him to briefly put aside the biography of Ulysses S. Grant that he was reading. And actors are professionally allowed and obliged to be obsessive students of human behavior. It's been going on for a long time. In speaking to the actors visiting him, Hamlet says that the attempt to portray human beings accurately, to be a mirror, has been the actor's goal "both at the first and now," and indeed what actors are always struggling to do in every scene they play is to make what they do seem believably like real life, no matter how unlike any situation in real life the situation depicted in the scene may be, no matter how unlike a real person the character they're playing may be, and no matter how dissimilar to the words spoken by real people the dialogue may be.

So you now have in your hands a collection of essays, written over a period of thirty-five years, in which I'm brooding about the world and even occasionally about the "world of make-believe" that I've had the privilege of living in. And naturally the essays paint a picture of me, of my life, and also of the strange period I've lived through and the shock of living through it. Because it's all been a shock, it wasn't what I'd grown up expecting, and I'm still shocked.

The experience of living through the last ten or twenty years has had its own special shocks. Some of the very tendencies that our parents felt they had driven off of the earth forever have crawled back onto the planet and amassed enormous power. More and more people, and more governmental "leaders," and more entire countries, have joyfully embraced, as their guiding political principles, sadism, injustice, and inventive forms of cruelty towards the weak. At the same time, for reasons that are mysterious to ordinary people, the world's money has flowed upwards towards a tiny group of individuals.

For me personally, it was a period in which I thought less about "Who am I?" and more about "What is this species that I seem to belong to?" (You can see this in particular in my longest essay, *Night Thoughts*.) But the two questions in fact are very closely related, because I think that the most striking thing about "me" is the way "I" lead two parallel lives at the same time. One life is the life of my thoughts. And my thoughts are about the suffering and death of my fellow human creatures and increasingly, because I've changed, and I care about things that at one time I never even considered, about the suffering and death of birds, the disappearance of butterflies and other fellow creatures of the earth who are not human, and even the catastrophes befalling lakes and glaciers that were never alive and have no feelings and that I've never visited and never will visit. But at the same time my other life is the life of my "self," which runs parallel to the life of my thoughts but is chaotically discordant with it. My self doesn't seem to change in response to my thoughts. Its priorities remain frighteningly the same as they've always been. While I eat my breakfast I'm usually watching on my computer a heart-breaking report about starving children, and it's awful, and I'm upset, but if while I'm watching the report I taste a slice of the loaf of bread that I absentmindedly pulled from the bread shelf of the supermarket the night before, and I don't enjoy the taste of the bread, I will angrily throw my slice of bread into the trash, and I'll throw the entire loaf of bread into the trash as well, because I simply have to enjoy the food I eat. There's no point in saving the rest of the loaf to eat later, because I'm never going to eat it. I don't eat food that I don't enjoy. It's as if out of my left eye I'm watching the children trying to extract nutrition from grass and leaves, and out of my right eye I'm watching myself throwing the bread into the trash, and the stereoscopic image is sickening. My thoughts are all about the starving children, and my thoughts bombard the self, but the self keeps marching forward, the way legend tells us Rasputin did after being repeatedly shot.

This personal drama isn't totally unrelated to what's been going on with our species as a whole in the last couple of decades.

To me it's interesting to realize that if we had the ability to take a trip back to the earth as it was, say, two million years ago, we might perhaps catch a glimpse of some of the ancient versions of horses, pigs, or apes, but from what we saw we'd be unlikely to guess that one day a single species would develop that would come to dominate the entire earth, and if we'd been informed that one species would indeed rise up above all the others, it's very unlikely that we would have been able to guess that that species would be descended from one of the early apes.

If we had been told, though, about a dominant species that would one day arise, perhaps we would have correctly guessed that it would be a species that had an appetite for domination. And could the act of domination itself be so exciting, perhaps, that when creatures achieve supremacy they become momentarily incapacitated, blind to the landscape surrounding them? Well then, perhaps it makes sense that the species that would dominate the world would also turn out to be a species that would destroy the world. In any event, the years of my life have been the years in which this horrible possibility, the destruction of the world by humanity, which at first was a prospect so awful that all of humanity joined together to prevent it, began to be a reality that a huge segment of humanity seemed to join together to accept. In other words, at the beginning of my life (I was born in 1943), the atomic bomb was created, but, after the unspeakable atrocities of Hiroshima and Nagasaki, the countries and the governments that developed and controlled the dreadful weapons, despite their fear of each other and their rivalry and their animosity and their strongly-held beliefs, nonetheless refrained, as of this writing, from using the weapons. But then, a mere half-century or so after the invention of the bomb, it was revealed that by coincidence (or was it a coincidence? it had to be, and yet it couldn't be) humanity had come up with a second technique by which it could end almost all life on earth, and this second technique was the simpler technique of systematically and directly poisoning the atmosphere, the climate, the air, the soil, the water, the birds, the fish, and the animals. The process of destruction of the conditions necessary for life on the planet had of course been going on in a gradual way since the industrial revolution, and even before that, but when humanity was finally brought to understand what was happening, people did not join together to stop it. On the contrary, the apparently infinite greed of the disturbed individuals who owned the engines of destruction—the executives and shareholders of the huge corporations—made it impossible for them to change course, and at the same time the great majority of the middle class people in the wealthy countries of the world declined to intervene. The truth is that they were so hopelessly addicted to the material comforts that seemed to provide a balm for their painful confusion and unhappiness that they were unwilling to risk the changes that were necessary if the poisoning process was to be halted. And so the process continues moving forward, not unlike the way my "self" continues moving forward. The species as a whole is in a way thinking, "Hm, we're going under." But the "self" of the species is saying, "I have to eat enjoyable slices of bread this morning, so leave me alone, I'm having my breakfast."

If history were predictable, if history followed a straight line, so that today's trends would simply continue in the same direction forever, until—well, no one wants to think about what would happen. But the good news is that history is not predictable. At least so far it never has been. And human beings, individually or as a group, are not predictable. Even the selfishness of the self is not predictable. Simone Weil didn't really need to go to work in a factory. Karl Marx was a brilliant man—he could have made a good living if he'd devoted himself to becoming a professor instead of writing the things he wanted to write. Martin Luther King, Jr. might be living today as an honored 91-year-old Baptist minister if he had taken a more moderate approach in his speeches and sermons. And why did Prince Gautama give up his riches? We don't know. But the essays in this book draw inspiration from the unexpected and unexplained developments that make it impossible for us to fully describe or define what people are like. Our attempts to see the limits of "human nature" always fail.

Sometimes the truth is worse than what we'd thought, but sometimes it's better. Despite the arc of disillusionment that might seem to be the shape of my years on earth, I want us to fight for survival.

DEDICATION TO THE BOOK *ESSAYS*, 2009

To Jonathan Schell and Deborah Eisenberg. In meditation (J.S.) and in fiction (D.E.): reality, truth, accepting it all; but then—intense, passionate dreams about extraordinary cities, a world where people live in harmony.

1951—talks on the state of the world begin with J.S. after eighth birthday party

1972—meet D.E.—shocked by her views—discussion of China leads to tears

Introduction to *Essays*
2009

The human community is carved up into "individuals." Why? Presumably because it's helped us to survive, because a sleeping dog can easily be kicked, but it's hard to damage a large group of flies. I honestly don't know. At any rate, I didn't ask to be an individual, but I find I am one, and by definition I occupy a space that no other individual occupies, or in other words, for what it's worth, I have my own point of view. I'm not proud to be me, I'm not excited to be me, but I find that I *am* me, and like most other individuals, I send out little signals, I tell everyone else how everything looks from where I am. I have more free time than a lot of individuals, so, instead of talking, I sometimes write. My friends Anthony and Brenda found my signals interesting, so Anthony asked me to collect them into a book.

I've always somewhat hated being "me" and only me. I wrote my first play at the age of ten, fifty-five years ago, and I've always found it a fantastic relief to imagine I know what things would be like from the point of view of other individuals and to send out signals from where I actually am *not*. Playwrights never need to write from the place where they are. Unlike the fiction writer who says, as himself, "Fred woke up in his bed that cloudy Sunday," a playwright can spend a lifetime writing without ever speaking from his own location.

I've passed my life largely in a fantasy world. My personal life is lived as "me," but my professional life is lived as other people. In other words, when I go to the office, I lie down, dream, and become "someone else." That's my job.

I've worked in the theatre since 1970. I've written plays and a few screenplays, in each one of which a person who isn't me speaks, and then another person who isn't me replies, and then a third one enters or the first one speaks again, and so it goes until the end of the piece. I've even worked as a professional actor, speaking out loud as if I were someone not myself. And perhaps it's disturbing or frightening how easy it is to become "someone else," to say the words of "someone else." It really doesn't feel odd at all, I have to tell you.

Every once in a while, though, I like to take a break from fantasyland, and I go off to the place called Reality for a brief vacation. It's happened a dozen or so times in the course of my life. I've looked at the world from my own point of view, and I've written these essays. I've written essays about reality, the world, and I've even written a few essays about the dream-world of "art" in which I normally dwell. In a bold mood I've brooded once or twice on the question, Where do the dreams go, and what do they do, in the world of the real?

My congenital inability to take the concept of the inviolable "self" seriously—my lack of certainty about who I am, where I am, and what my "characteristics" are—has led me to a certain skepticism, a certain detachment, when people in my vicinity are reviling the evil and alien Other, because I feel that very easily I could become that Other, and so could the reviler. And this has had an effect on my view of the world.

I grew up listening to discussions about the world, and in school I studied history and politics and even a little elementary economics. My parents were completely (some might say excessively) assimilated American Jews whose own parents (said with only a moderate degree of certainty to have been born in Sweden, England, Germany, and possibly Canada) were probably all of Eastern European or Russian origin, or in other words, saved from a harsh destiny by the existence of the United States of America. My mother and father, fortunate members of the bourgeoisie, were American liberals of the old school. They never described the United States as "the greatest country in the world" as many politicians did. They were passionately close to their French friends and their English friends and presided over a living room in which people from India, Poland, Italy, and Czechoslovakia were constant visitors, and they adored and admired Adlai Stevenson. From an early age, I remember going with my mother to the gorgeous, modern United Nations buildings on our own island of Manhattan and buying holiday cards from UNICEF in the United Nations gift shop. (As a Jewish atheist, my mother was one of the world's most loyal devotees of Christmas, and she loved Advent calendars, Christmas trees, and Christmas cards.) Mother loved UNICEF, the United Nations Children's Emergency Fund, which helped poor children all over the world, and she loved the United Nations; and, to her, being an American meant being a person who loved the United Nations and was a friend to poor children all over the world, like Eleanor Roosevelt and Adlai Stevenson.

When not totally preoccupied with my own problems, I feel some of the emotions my mother felt toward those poor children all over the world. But my earliest essay, "Morality," from 1985 (I was just over forty years old when I wrote it) shows me slowly seeing, as it appeared out of the mist, the outline of my own figure as a character in their story. It turned out that my role was sinister, dreadful, but for my first forty years I hadn't realized that. My ignorance about my own involvement in the story of the children allowed me to think, Yes, the conditions in the world are terrible, certainly—but I still could feel that the topic could be discussed in a leisurely manner. When one hasn't noticed that it's one's own boot that's standing on the suffering person's neck, one can be calmly sympathetic to the suffering person and hope that over time things will work out well for them.

I never became as nice as my mother. But by the time I was forty-five I understood a few things that she'd overlooked. I suppose I'm something like what my mother would have been if she'd gone down into her basement and stumbled on Eleanor Roosevelt murdering babies there.

The schizophrenic nature of this book (essays on war and death and essays on the windowless miniature world of theatre) gives a pretty good picture of my own mind. Born by most definitions into the ruling class, I was destined to live a comfortable life. And to spend one's life as a so-called "creative artist" is probably the most comfortable, cozy, and privileged life that a human being can live on this earth—the most "bourgeois" life, if one uses that phrase to describe a life that is so comfortable that no one living it would want to give it up. To lie in bed and watch words bump together until they become sentences is a form of hedonism, whether the words and sentences glorify society and the status quo or denounce them. It's very agreeable to live like that, even if people don't like your work, criticize you, whatever. So I've always been tempted to turn off the radio and forget the world, but I'm not quite enough of a hedonist to forget it entirely and forever. I'm unable to totally forget the world—but I still haven't (yet) become a compassionate enough person to leave my bed for more than a moment in order to devote myself to *changing* the world or alleviating the suffering of my fellow human beings.

In other words, I've been divided, like this book. When I was fifteen, my brain was feverish with the work of Dostoevsky and James Joyce. But by the time I was twenty I'd turned against art, I planned to spend my life as a civil servant, helping humanity, and I would no more have dreamed that I'd one day work in the theatre than that I'd one day become a champion racing car driver. Five years later I'd fallen hard for art again, and I was loyal to art for twenty years. Then its immorality became intolerable to me, and I turned against it again, though I failed to find, as I looked around me, anything else that I wanted to do. At any rate, the oscillations continued, their pattern unpredictable and indecipherable to me.

Not surprisingly, my own ambivalence leaves me totally in awe of those amazing people whose concerns and passions have stayed constant and undimmed throughout their lives. I find I do need models or heroes to guide me on my journey through the world, and this need, combined with my shaky grasp on who I find "myself" to be, led me not merely to seek out and interview the poet Mark Strand and the political philosopher Noam Chomsky, but to believe, against the evidence, that they *were me*, and so I insisted that these interviews were essays of mine and had to be included as part of this book. Of course one could say that no one person could *be* both Noam Chomsky and Mark Strand, not merely because it's miraculous that anyone ever was remarkable enough to be *either* of them, but because their lives seem to point in opposite directions. That doesn't seem to stop me from wanting to be both of them at the same time, and it doesn't seem to stop me from refusing to accept that their lives are contradictory. Somehow poetry and the search for a more just order on earth are not contradictory, and rational thought and dreams are not contradictory, and there may be something necessary, as well as ridiculous, in the odd activity of racing back and forth on the bridge between reality and the world of dreams.

April 2009, New York City

After the Destruction of the World Trade Center
November 2001

To: The Foreign Policy Therapist
From: The United States of America, November 12, 2001

Dear Foreign Policy Therapist,

I don't know what to do. I want to be safe. I want safety. But I have a terrible problem: It all began several weeks ago when I lost several thousand loved ones to a horrible terrorist crime. I feel an overwhelming need to apprehend and punish those who committed this unbearably cruel act, but they designed their crime in such a diabolical fashion that I cannot do so, because they arranged to be killed themselves while committing the crime, and they are now all dead. I feel in my heart that none of these men, however, could possibly have planned this crime themselves and that another man, who is living in a cave in Afghanistan, must surely have done so. At any rate I know that some people he knows knew some of the people who committed the crime and possibly gave them some money. I feel an overwhelming need to kill this man in the cave, but the location of the cave is unknown to me, and so it's impossible to find him. He's been allowed to stay in the cave, however, by the fanatical rulers of the country where the cave is, Afghanistan, so I feel an overwhelming need to kill those rulers. As they've moved from place to place, though, I haven't found them, but I've succeeded in finding and killing many young soldiers who guarded them and shepherds who lived near them. Nonetheless, I do not feel any of the expected "closure," and in fact I'm becoming increasingly depressed and am obsessed with nameless fears. Can you help me?

To: The United States of America
From: The Foreign Policy Therapist

Dear United States,

In psychological circles, we call your problem "denial." You cannot face your real problem, so you deny that it exists and create instead a different problem that you try to solve. Meanwhile, the real problem, denied and ignored, becomes more and more serious. In your case, your real problem is simply the way that millions and millions of people around the world feel about you.

Who are these people? They share the world with you—one single world, which works as a unified mechanism. These people are the ones for whom the mechanism's current way of working—call it the status quo—offers a life of anguish and servitude. They're well aware that this status quo, which for them is a prison, is for you (or for the privileged among you), on the contrary, so close to a paradise that you will never allow their lives to change. These millions of people are in many cases uneducated—to you they seem unsophisticated—and yet they still somehow know that you have played an enormous role in keeping this status quo in place. And so they know you as the enemy. They feel they have to fight you. Some of them hate you. And some will gladly die in order to hurt you—in order to stop you.

They know where the fruits of the planet, the oil and the spices, are going. And when your actions cause grief in some new corner of the world, they know about it. And when you kill people who are poor and desperate, no matter what explanation you give for what you've done, their anger against you grows. You can't kill all these millions of people, but almost any one of them, in some way, some place, or to some degree, can cause damage to you.

But here's a strange fact about these people whom you consider unsophisticated: Most of the situations in the world in which they perceive "injustice" are actually ones in which you yourself would see injustice if you yourself weren't so deeply involved in creating the situations. Even though they may dress differently and live differently, their standards of justice seem oddly similar to yours.

Your problem, ultimately, can only be solved over decades, through a radical readjustment of the way you think and behave. If the denial persists, you are sure to continue killing more poor and desperate people, causing the hatred against you to grow, until at a certain point there will be no hope for you. But it's not too late. Yes, there are some among your current enemies who can no longer be reached by reason. Yes, there are some who are crazy. But most are not. Most people are not insane. If you do change, it is inevitable that over time people will know that you have changed, and their feelings about you will also change, and the safety you seek will become a possibility.

The Quest for Superiority
2008

When I was five years old, I had a small room of my own, with a record-player and records and shelves full of books. I listened to music, I thought up different kinds of stories, and I played with paper and crayons and paint.

Now I've grown up, and thank God things have mostly gone on as before—the paper, the stories—it's pretty much the same. I've been allowed to become a professional maker of art, I've become a writer, and I dwell in the mansion of arts and letters.

When I was a child, I didn't know that the pieces of paper I used had been made by anybody. I certainly didn't know that almost everything I touched had been made by people who were poor, people who worked in factories or on farms or places like that. In fact I'd never met anyone who worked in a factory or on a farm. I'd frequently met people who *owned* factories and farms, because they lived all around us in the huge houses I could see from my window, although I wasn't aware then that the houses *were* huge because the people who lived in them paid very low salaries to their employees, while paying themselves enormous sums. Our wealthy neighbors were really like the giants in a fantastic tale, giants who were superior to others because they could spin gold out of human suffering.

Well, it turns out that I still live in the same neighborhood, because that's where the mansion of arts and letters is located. So I still can see giants when I look out my window, and the funny thing is that pretty much all of us in the mansion of arts and letters actually live off the money we get from these giants.

Isn't that funny? You know, they buy the tickets to our shows, they buy our books and paintings, they support the universities where we teach, there are gifts and grants—it all comes out of the gold they've spun. And we live with them, we share the streets with them, and we're all protected by the same cops.

But you see, some of the people who *don't* live in the neighborhood—the ones our neighbors don't pay well, or treat well?—some of those people are out of control, they're so miserable, so desperate, they're out of their minds, they're very *threatening*, so it turns out we need more than cops. We actually have a large army as well, and a navy and an air force, plus the F.B.I., Coast Guard, Central Intelligence Agency, and marines—oy. It turned out that simply in order to be secure and protect our neighborhood, we needed an empire.

Some of us who live in the mansion of arts and letters are a bit touchy about our relationship to our wealthy neighbors. Bob, for example—he's a painter who lives down the hall from me—he refuses to bow to them when they pass him in the street, but, you know—they buy his paintings just the same. For me, though, it's my relationship with the poor people *outside* the neighborhood that I sometimes brood about in the middle of the night. It's the fact that so many of them are in agony that's in a way thought-provoking.

One evening last week, a friend and I went to a somewhat inexpensive restaurant, and the waiter who served us was in such a state of agitation or anxiety about God knows what that he didn't even look at us. And so I was thinking about the fact that in more expensive restaurants, the staff is usually trained to focus their attention on the pleasure of the diners, not on their own problems. In fact, the waiters in more expensive restaurants are invited to be friendly, amusing, to make funny remarks about their lives, to let us diners get to know them a little. But in the *most* expensive restaurants, the really fancy ones, we don't get to know the waiters at all. The waiters in those restaurants don't make funny remarks. They do their work with such discretion that they're barely noticed. And people compliment them by saying that they're unobtrusive.

Actually that's quite a good word for all those people whom we don't know and don't think about much but who serve us and make the things we need and whose lives we actually dominate: "the unobtrusives." And the interesting thing I've noticed is that in those very expensive restaurants, we don't talk with the waiters, but we enjoy their presence enormously. We certainly wouldn't want them to be replaced by robots or by conveyer belts that would carry our food to us while we sat in the dining room completely alone. No, we want them there, these silent waiters, these—"unobtrusives."

It's obviously a characteristic of human beings that we like to feel superior to others. But our problem is that we're *not* superior. We like the sensation of being served by others and feeling superior to them, but if we're forced to get to know the people who serve us, we quickly see that they're in fact just like us. And then we become uncomfortable—uncomfortable and *scared*, because if *we* can see that we're just the same, well, *they* might too, and if they did, they might become terribly, terribly angry, because why should they be serving us? So that's why we prefer not to talk to waiters.

A king feels the very same way, I'd have to imagine. He doesn't really want to get to know his subjects, but he nonetheless enjoys the fact that he has them. He finds it enjoyable to be told, "Your Majesty, you have ten thousand subjects." And in fact he finds it even more enjoyable to be told, "Your Majesty, you have a million subjects," even though he may never see them. The subjects are in the background of his life. They're in the background of his life, and yet they provide the meaning of his life. Without his subjects, he wouldn't be king.

Some people like to feel superior because once they were made to feel inferior. Others, including myself, were told constantly in their early days that they *were* superior and now find themselves to be hopelessly addicted. So, if I get into a conversation, for example, with a person who knows nothing about me, I immediately start to experience a sort of horrible tension, as if my head were being squashed, because the person I'm talking to is unaware of my superiority. Well, I have at my disposal an arsenal of indicators of superiority that I can potentially deploy—I can casually allude to certain schools I attended, to my artistic work, to the elegant street on which I grew up—but if, by analogy to some of those Tantric exercises one reads about, I attempt to follow the counterintuitive path of not revealing any of these clues—well, it's simply interesting to observe that I can rarely manage to hold out for as long as ten minutes before forcing my interlocutor to learn the truth about me.

Weirdly, it turns out to be possible for a person to feel superior because someone somehow *connected* to them has been raised up above others—a friend, an acquaintance, a parent, a child—and the connection can be even vaguer than that. I have to admit, I take a certain pride in Gustav Mahler's symphonies—after all, he was Jewish, and so am I. And Emily Dickinson was born in the United States, just like me. Incidentally, one unmistakable way to know you're superior to someone is to beat them up. And just as I feel rather distinguished if a writer from the United States wins the Nobel Prize, I also feel stronger and more important because my country's army happens to dominate the world. The king doesn't need to meet his subjects in order to enjoy his dominion over them, and I don't need to go to Iraq to know that there are people all over the world, a great number of quiet "unobtrusives," who experience a feeling of stomach-turning terror when they see soldiers wearing the uniform of my country approaching their door in the middle of the night. Now, let's admit that some of the rougher people who seem to thrive in our country, people like George Bush or Dick Cheney, for example, may perhaps take actual pleasure from the thought of our country's soldiers smashing in the door of some modest house in some godforsaken region of the planet, forcing a family to huddle on the floor, administering kicks in the face to anyone they like. Perhaps there may even be a modest clerk in a bank in Kansas or a quiet housewife on a farm in Idaho who feels a bit of enjoyment at a thought like that. But what bothers me more is that although I have nothing but contempt for imperial adventures, I've marched in the streets to demonstrate for peace, and I don't make it a practice to wink or joke about the brutal actions of brutal men, I can't deny that in spite of myself I derive some sense of superiority from being a citizen of a country that can act brutally with impunity and can't be stopped. I feel quite different from the way I know I would feel if I were a citizen of Grenada, Tonga, or Mauritius.

My feeling of superiority, and the sense of well-being that comes from that, increases with the number of poor people on the planet whose lives are dominated by me or my proxies and whom I nonetheless can completely ignore. I like to be reminded of these poor people, the unobtrusives, and then I like to be reminded of my lack of interest in them. For example, while I eat my breakfast each morning, I absolutely love to read my morning newspaper, because in the first few pages the newspaper tells me how my country treated all the unobtrusives on the day before—deaths, beatings, torture, what have you—and then, as I keep turning the pages, the newspaper reminds me how unimportant the unobtrusives are to me, and it tries to tempt me in its articles on shirts to consider different shirts that I might want to wear, and then it goes on, as I turn the pages, to try to coax me into sampling different forms of cooking, and then to experience different plays or films, different types of vacations . . .

It's become second nature to me to use the quiet crushing of the unobtrusives as a sort of almost inaudible background music to my daily life. Like those people who grow bizarrely nervous if they don't have a recording of something or other quietly playing on their sound system at dinnertime, we've become dependent over the course of decades on hearing the faint murmur of cries and groans as we eat, shop, and live.

How will the world change? Believe me, those who are now unobtrusive have their own ideas about how the situation might improve. But in the middle of the night I wonder: Can we in the mansion of arts and letters play a part? Could we reduce the destructiveness of the people we know? Could we possibly use the dreams we create to lure our friends in another direction? Because it's valuable to remember that the feeling of superiority is not the only source of human satisfaction. Imperial dreams are not the only dreams. I've known people, for example, who've derived satisfaction from collecting seashells. And sometimes I think of a woman I knew a long time ago who seemed to be terribly happy, although her life consisted of not much more than getting up each day, playing with the cat, reading a mystery, eating an agreeable sandwich for lunch, then taking a walk in the afternoon. No wealthy giant eating dishes costing hundreds of dollars could ever have enjoyed a meal more than this woman seemed to enjoy her simple sandwiches—so what was her secret? And what about Edgar, who gets such pleasure out of working as a nurse, or Tom, who finds such nourishment teaching children in school? Jane's need for superiority seems fully satisfied if a friend admires one of her drawings. And Edna's overjoyed if she wins at cards. People can make a life, it seems, out of love—out of gardening, out of sex, friendship, the company of animals, the search for enlightenment, the enjoyment of beauty. Wait—isn't that our particular province?

Beauty can be important in a person's life. And people beguiled by the beautiful are less dangerous to others than those obsessed by the thought of supremacy. If an afternoon of reading poetry has given me a feeling of profound well-being, I don't then need to go out into the street and seek satisfaction by strangling prostitutes. Art can be central in a person's life. If the art we create is beautiful enough, will people be so drawn to looking at it that they'll leave behind their quest for power? Beauty really is more enjoyable than power. A poem really is more enjoyable than an empire, because a poem doesn't hate you. The defense of privilege, the center of our lives for such a long time, is grim, exhausting. We're exhausted from holding on to things, exhausted from trying not to see those unobtrusive people we're kicking away, whose suffering is actually unbearable to us.

In the mansion of arts and letters, we live like children, running and playing up and down the hallways all day and all night. We fill room after room with the things we make. After our deaths, we'll leave behind our poems, drawings, and songs, made for our own pleasure, and we won't know if they'll be allowed to help in the making of a better world.

Aesthetic Preferences
2008

It's easier to sleep if your head is elevated, and so people use pillows. If you want to attach one piece of cloth to another piece of cloth, a sewing machine can be extremely helpful, and that's why Isaac M. Singer made sewing machines. But why do people make and use what we call "artistic" objects?

It's a question that seems particularly puzzling if you make such objects yourself, in a way devoting your life to it, without quite knowing why you're doing it.

George Gershwin might possibly have wondered to himself, "Why do I write songs?" and yet, as soon as he wrote them, many, many of his fellow humans were eager to sing them, and others were dying to listen to them, and when they heard them, they all felt better and happier. So even though, in a way, those facts don't quite answer the original question—they don't quite explain Gershwin's drive to write music—still, in another way, what more of an answer could Gershwin possibly have wanted?

Everyone knows that if you're hungry and depressed, a little ice cream can bring a moment of relief, and that's why we like it. I presented my early plays to the world with many of the same feelings that Gershwin probably felt when he presented his songs—in each case I had given my all and done my best to make something that I found pleasing. Nonetheless, my first professional production in New York (in 1975) provoked a level of hostility in its small audience that was seriously disturbing. In my second production, the anger of the audience seemed to diminish a bit, but they seemed stricken and miserable instead—hurt, or baffled.

Every day I wake up wondering what has happened to those early plays of mine in the intervening years. They haven't caught on, apparently, even after all this time. And the years I spent writing them—what were those years? Were they like the years that recovered alcoholics describe—"lost years" spent wandering in a desperate haze from one night's incomprehensible encounter with someone or other to the next night's horrible barroom brawl?

Not long ago, I made a film with a group of people, and we'd poured a significant portion of our lives into making it, along with quite a bit of thought and passion, and finally it was shown at a film festival. And when the screening of the film was over, a moderator asked the audience if anyone had any questions for the filmmakers. Almost instantly, a man spoke up from the center of the auditorium. "Yes, I have a question," he said in a loud voice. "What was the point of that?" Now, let's note that his question could have meant two different things. He might have been wondering what the point was for us in making the film. Or he might have been asking what point there could possibly have been for him in watching it. But in a way, I feel that my whole life seems to revolve around the fact that I'm crawling through the streets every day unable to answer either version of that question about anything I do.

You have to understand, I do read my plays myself every few years, including the ones that people have liked least. I read them, I change a few words, I improve a few lines, and I'm surprised once again that so few people liked them. "What *is* it about me and all those other people?" I think to myself. I like orange juice, and so do they. I like the performances of Roseanne Barr and Robert De Niro, and so do they. But I like my own plays, and they don't. Why is that?

People always say that "tastes differ," and that that's just a fact. A lot of people like spinach. Many fewer like dandelion greens. When certain people take their clothes off in public, they're worshipped and rewarded, while others are arrested or taken to an insane asylum. But if you have a stake in the answer, it's hard not to ask, "Why the spinach? Why not the greens?" Is there no comprehensible reason that the spinach is more popular?

Of course there *are* answers, but you'd have to devote your life to a scientific study of preferences in vegetables in order to begin to find out about preferences in vegetables, and it would be the same with all other areas of preference.

Leaving aside my own plays, I've always been curious why, in comparison to most people I know, I enjoy plays in general so much. I can't, obviously, answer that question either.

I do like plays, though. There's something so chaotic about them. And I like to write the text that appears in a play, that is part of a play. For me, a play is a wonderful pileup of bodies, lights, sets, gestures, clothes, nudity, music, dance, and running through it all and driving it all is a stream of words, sentences. Words and sentences are (to me) aesthetic materials, and a purpose that I think one would have to call aesthetic can certainly be the governing element in writing a play. One plays with sentences the way a child plays with matches—because they're unpredictable. In fact, sentences make up a sort of jungle in which I seem to be living. And somehow an artistic object comes into being, that is, an object that exists for the purpose of being contemplated.

And the contemplation of an artistic object can induce a sort of daytime dream, one might say. And perhaps it's somewhat odd for a play to have that intention, at least in comparison to a painting, for example. Agnes Martin's paintings put the viewer into a trance, while Bertolt Brecht's plays were specifically designed to wake people up. But Strindberg thought that a play could be like a dream.

I wonder if the daytime dreams induced by artistic objects may not be really rather necessary for people, as nighttime dreams unquestionably are. If they weren't necessary, then why would every culture on earth invent music, songs, poetry, what have you? Perhaps it's the case that, in order to live, we must process our experience first rationally, and then irrationally. But if such dreams are actually necessary in fact, that goes some way to explaining the horrible atmosphere that has hovered in various rooms in which my plays have been performed. In other words, at night we can all create for ourselves the dreams that we need, but the creation of the artistic objects that stimulate our daytime dreams is contracted out to a particular group of people, and in our society it's a self-appointed group. So naturally the various dreams that we dream at night are not criticized by anybody—there are no reviewers in the Land of Nod—nor do we need to defend our dreams or make any claims for them. But as we all find ourselves in the frustrating situation that most of the artistic objects we need and depend on for our daytime dreams must be made by other people, it's not surprising that we're finicky, critical, and sometimes even angry when these objects are presented to us—we're constantly complaining, like diners in a restaurant who repeatedly send bad-tasting dishes back to the kitchen. And then, perhaps inevitably, centuries ago, analysts of art brought the concepts of "good" and "bad" into the conversation, and most of us, as irritable diners, frequently use this vocabulary in discussing our artistic meals, although it often merely adds to the prevailing confusion, because a parsnip is not really a "bad" carrot, it's a different vegetable.

So. What type of dreams do you enjoy? There are clearly different categories of dreams that vie for primacy in each human soul. Some are dreams of conquest, victory, or revenge. Others are dreams of sensuality, beauty, joy, kindness, and love. Artistic objects are not brainwashing machines. They have influence, not power. But I think we're influenced by our daytime dreams, just as much as we're influenced by our family and friends and our personal experiences. So to me it's reasonable to think that a world in which Chuang Tzu and George Eliot are widely read will be less dangerous than a world in which people read only sadistic stories or military magazines.

Certain theorists definitely disagree with that opinion. Actually, there are people who dwell almost obsessively on the fact that an exposure to "art" did not prevent certain famous men from doing horrible things. I feel I've been frequently reminded, for example, that the Nazi leader Reinhard Heydrich played Mozart on the violin during the same period in which he planned the extermination of the Jews. But my speculation on this, if I may offer one, is that, perhaps because of his history and who he was, Commander Heydrich did not fully absorb the human possibilities that others have grasped through listening to the music of Mozart. Similarly, the young English major Seung-Hui Cho killed thirty-two people in a famous massacre at a college in Virginia, even though a kindly professor of English had given him private tutorials in creative writing and had even tried to speak to him sympathetically about his own problems. She did her best, but Cho was too deeply trapped in the quicksand of his own mind, and the lessons in creative writing didn't save him. He didn't hear enough, or understand enough, of what his teacher was trying to tell him. Mozart, being a composer of music rather than a supernatural creature from outer space, was not up to the task of convincing Reinhard Heydrich to get off the path he was on and move to another one. But just as the failure of Cho's teacher can hardly lead us to say that no kindly teacher has ever helped or saved a student, so it seems preposterous to leap from Mozart's inability to reconstruct Reinhard Heydrich to the claim that composers, painters, and writers have not influenced the world by offering humanity their wisdom and their vision of what life could be.

Dreams can help, although they don't make their points in a direct way, and sometimes no one can say for sure exactly what their points really are. Dreams can even agitate for change, or for a better world, sometimes simply by offering people a glimpse of something agreeable that might be pursued—or crystallizing into a vivid nightmare something awful that ought to be avoided. Dreams are actually involved in a serious battle. Despite a certain lightness in their presentation, they're not joking.

Patriotism
1991

In July 1991, the Nation *magazine asked various people to submit brief reflections on "patriotism."*

"Patriotism" can seem to be as harmless as the love of certain musical instruments, food, a landscape. Certain personalities from one's own country can seem so charming, so delightful. But "patriotism" always seems to mean: If you feel a fondness for your country, then it ought to be worth it to you to do "x."

Patriotism is considered to be an emotion a person ought to feel. But why? Why is it nobler to love your own country than to love someone else's? Why is it particularly wonderful to think that the place you're from is the greatest in the world? Why should individuals speak in the first person plural about "our ideals" and "the things we believe"?

If certain great figures from our country's past have had valuable insights, by all means let's be inspired by them. But let's not make a fetish out of it. The United States is a monster that must be stopped, controlled. It's too elaborate to say (again and again), "We must change our current behavior because it violates our noble traditions." The historical point is probably untrue, and anyway, it doesn't matter. What's necessary is to change the behavior. We don't need to be flattered while we're doing it, and in any case, even if we *have* some noble ancestors, that wouldn't mean that *we* have any particular merit.

For citizens of small, weak countries, patriotism might be connected to a yearning for justice. For people who are despised, who despise themselves, more self-esteem might be a good thing. But for people who already are in love with themselves, who worship themselves, who consider themselves more important than others, more self-esteem is not needed. Self-knowledge would be considerably more helpful.

"Morality"
1985

When I was around thirteen, I was sitting on a sofa with an older woman, and she said to me rather fiercely, "You don't understand this now, but when you get older, you'll come to appreciate the importance of comfort." This did turn out to be true. At that time, I really didn't have much to be comforted about or comforted from, so naturally comfort didn't matter to me then. And now it does. And the older I get, the more I long to feel really comfortable. But I've also come to realize that an awful lot of preparatory work must be undertaken before that particular feeling can begin to exist, and I've learned, too, how all that effort can count for nothing if even one tiny element of the world around me refuses to fit into its necessary place. Yes, I'm at home in my lovely apartment, I'm sitting in my cozy rocking chair, there are flowers on the table, tranquil colors of paint on the walls. But if I've caught a fever and I'm feeling sick, or if a nearby faucet has developed a leak, or if a dog in the courtyard six floors below me is barking, the unity of my peaceful scene is spoiled, and comfort flies out the window. And unfortunately, what in fact prevents me more than anything else from feeling really comfortable—whether I'm leaning back against a soft banquette in a pleasant restaurant or spending a drowsy morning in bed propped up on three or four pillows—is actually the well-intentioned ethical training I received as a child.

My parents brought me up to believe in "morality"—an approach toward life that was based on the paradoxical concept of "self-restraint." "Morality" essentially described how a person would behave if he believed all human beings to be equally real, if he cared equally about all human beings, even though one of them happened, in fact, to be himself. And undoubtedly there were certain individuals who had a special gift for morality, the way some people had a gift for music or pleasure. But we, for the most part, lacked that gift, so we were taught principles about how to behave.

And at the same time, we were taught that in order to live morally, it was necessary to seek out accurate knowledge about things. Maybe it could sometimes be "right," for example, to kill another person. But if I acted impulsively and killed another person because of misperceived facts or erroneous suspicions, that would be "wrong."

But I realize now that this entire training in morality is a jarring element in the life I'm leading, and in my struggle to feel comfortable, to feel at ease, it functions rather like a dog whose barking never stops, a dog whose barking persists throughout the day and then continues regularly all night long. It is a perpetual irritation. Everything visible around me may be perfect and serene, but inside, there is this voice that never stops denouncing me. It does not fit in. Of course I'd be pleased if I could claim that all my relations with other people were in perfect harmony with the laws of morality—and as a matter of fact, in my daily interactions with my friends and colleagues and loved ones, I usually try to follow ethical precepts. But when I draw the curtains of perception a little bit wider and consider the fact that there are thousands and millions of people out there in the world, all quite real, as real as me, and that I have some sort of relation to every one of them, I have to admit that it would be hard to insist that all these relations of mine are truly obedient to those solemn laws.

In contrast to the African miner who works underground doing painfully difficult labor in terrifying conditions and then receives a minuscule reward, I have a life that is extremely pleasant. I have enough money to buy myself warm and comfortable shoes and sweaters; each Wednesday I pay a nice person to clean my apartment and keep it neat; and each April at tax time I pay my government to perform a similar service in the world outside. I pay it to try to keep the world more or less as it is, so that next year it will not suddenly be me who is working a seventy-hour week in some godforsaken pit or digging in some field under the burning sun. It's all terrific, but my problem is that my government is the medium through which I conduct my relationships with most of my fellow human beings, and I'm obliged to note that its actions don't conform to the principles of morality. Yes, I may be a friendly fellow to meet on the street, but I've found, through my government, a sneaky way to do some terrible things. And so this is why I feel a fantastic need to tear all that moral training out of my heart once and for all so that I can finally begin to enjoy the life that is spread out before me like a marvelous feast. And every time that a friend decides to abandon morality and set himself free, I find that I inwardly exult and rejoice, because it means there will be one less person to disapprove of me if I choose to do the same.

As I write these words, in New York City in 1985, more and more people who grew up around me are making this decision; they are throwing away their moral chains and learning to enjoy their true situation: Yes, they are admitting loudly and bravely, We live in beautiful homes, we're surrounded by beautiful gardens, our children are playing with wonderful toys, and our kitchen shelves are filled with wonderful food. And if there are people out there who are envious of us and who might even be tempted to break into our homes and take what we have, well then, part of our good fortune is that we can afford to pay guards to protect us. And if those who protect us need to hit people in the face with the butts of their rifles, or if they need perhaps even to turn around and shoot, they have our permission, and we only hope they'll do what they do with diligence and skill.

The amazing thing I've noticed about those friends of mine who've made that choice is that as soon as they've made it, they begin to blossom, to flower, because they are no longer hiding, from themselves or anyone else, the true facts about their own lives. They become very frank about human nature. They freely admit that man is a predatory creature, a hunter and a fighter, and they admit that it can warm a human's heart to trick an enemy, to make him cry, to make him do what he doesn't want to do, and even to make him crawl in the mud and die in agony. They admit that to manipulate people can be an art, and that to deceive people can be entertaining. They admit that there's a skill involved in playing life's game, and they admit that it's exciting to bully and threaten and outwit and defeat all the other people who are playing against you. And as they learn to admit these things, and they lose the habit of looking over their shoulders in fear at the disapproving ghosts of their parents and teachers, they develop the charm and grace that shine out from all people who are truly comfortable with themselves, who are not worried, who are not ashamed of their own actions. These are people who are free to love life exuberantly. They can enjoy a bottle of wine or a walk in the garden with unmixed pleasure, because they feel justified in having the bottle of wine, in having the garden. And if, by chance, they run into the laundress who takes care of their clothes, they can chat with her happily and easily, because they accept the fact that some people, themselves, happen to wear beautiful clothes, and others are paid to keep them clean. And, in fact, these people who accept themselves are people whose company everyone enjoys.

So there are those who live gracelessly in a state of discomfort because they allow themselves to be whipped on an hourly basis by morality's lash, and then there's another group of cheerful, self-confident people who've put morality aside for now, and they're feeling great, and it's fun to be with them. But if we decide that we *don't* need to see all people as equally real, and we come to believe that we ourselves and the groups we belong to are more real, we of course are making a factual mistake.

I was born during World War Two, and somehow I've spent a lot of time over the course of my life thinking about the character of Adolf Hitler, and one amazing thing about Hitler was the way his extraordinary self-confidence enabled him to expound his theories of the world to his aides and orderlies and secretaries at the dining room table night after night with no sense that he needed to keep checking to see if his theories were soundly grounded in facts. Hitler's boundless self-confidence enabled him to live each day as a tireless murderer; no weakness, no flagging energy, kept his knife from plunging into his victims hour after hour with mechanical ease.

Hitler was a man who was drawn to murder, to thinking about murder, to dwelling on murder. Particularly to dwelling on murder. Can we not imagine with what eager excitement he must have listened to the reports from the death camps, the crematoria, which he never in fact visited on a single occasion? But when we speak of dwelling on murder . . . that person standing over the daily newspaper—reading about the massacre, reading about the bloodbath, reading about the execution in a room in the prison—that person is me. And am I not in some part of myself identifying with the one in the story who is firing the machine gun at the innocent people, who is pulling the switch that sends the jolts of power through the prisoner strapped in the electric chair? And do I not also enjoy reading about those incredible scientists who are making the preparations for what we might do in some future nuclear or chemical or biological war that someday might take place? Do I not join them in picturing, with some small relish, the amazing effects that our different devices would have on possible victims? Is my blood not racing with abnormal speed as I read about these things? Is there not something trembling inside me? I know that these planners, these scientists, are not involved in killing. They're killing no one. But I see what they're doing—they're building the gas chambers, getting together the pellets of poison, assembling the rooms where the clothing and valuables will all be sorted, transporting the victims to convenient camps, and asking them to get undressed for the showers and disinfection that will soon follow. Of course, no one is putting people into the chambers. No one is pumping in the gas.

But wait a minute. Am I crazy now? What am I saying? Of course, I may have all sorts of dangerous impulses somewhere inside me, but the difference between Hitler and me is that there was nothing in Hitler that restrained him from following any of his insane impulses to their logical, insane conclusions—he was capable of doing anything at all, if given the chance—because he was utterly without connection to morality.

But I just was thinking about cutting my connection to morality also.

Yes, I was thinking about it. But I didn't do it. At least, I have no memory of doing it. Or was there actually some moment when I did do it, which I've now forgotten?

I don't feel very confident about my memory of my life. I know there was a time when I was not like Hitler. And my entire past feels so terribly close, it's as if I could reach out and touch it. Could I have become one of those people who remembers, as if it were yesterday, the time when principles of decency grew freshly in his heart, when a love for humanity set him off on his path in life, who still believes that each of his actions is driven and motivated by those very principles and that very love, but who in fact has become a coarse brute who abandoned love and principles a long time ago?

How could a person break his attachment to morality without noticing it, without feeling it, without remembering it? Could a perfectly decent person just turn into a coldhearted beast, a monster, and still feel pretty much the same?

Of course. A perfectly decent person can turn into a monster perfectly easily. And there's no reason why he would feel any different. Because the difference between a perfectly decent person and a monster is just a few thoughts. The perfectly decent person who follows a certain chain of reasoning, ever so slightly and subtly incorrect, becomes a perfect monster at the end of the chain.

Thoughts have extraordinary power in the human world, and yet they can behave so unpredictably. Familiar thoughts can lead us by the hand to very strange thoughts. And in a way, we're not as clever as our own thoughts, which have a peculiar habit of developing on their own and taking us to conclusions we never particularly wanted to reach. Within each thought, it seems, other thoughts are hidden, waiting to crawl out.

As the morning begins and I slowly turn my head to look at the clock on my bedside bookcase, my thoughts are already leaping and playing in my brain, ceaselessly spawning other thoughts, changing their shape, dividing in two and then dividing again, merging, dancing together in gigantic clumps. There's no end to the things that the thoughts will do if no one is paying any attention to them.

Our thoughts jump and fly. The world races forward. And meanwhile we're walking slowly around in a daze, trying to remember whether we're still connected to morality or not. False arguments, rapidly expressed, confuse us, seduce us, corrupt us. The chains of reasoning, of thinking, appeared to be sound. What was wrong? But we forget that thinking has its own pathology, and we sit in some room listening to a discussion, and something reasonable and admirable is said, and we nod our heads, and somehow we keep on nodding, and moments later we've agreed to something that would make our former selves turn purple with shame. But we sit there blankly, unaware that anything has happened. Why was it that we failed to notice the first signs of sickness in the argument? At the crucial moment, had our attention wandered? Why would that be? Are we particularly tired right now? Exhausted?

Our lives develop, and our thoughts change, and as our thoughts change, we change. We change each day in small steps, brief conversations, half-conscious moments of reflection, of doubt and resolution.

I stand at the door of my house, ready to defend the loved ones inside from the marauder lurking in the dark. As I steel myself to shoot the marauder, I say to myself, "I must be hard. Cold. Unsentimental." I repeat the litany a hundred times. And the next morning, when the marauder has not come—or the marauder has come, and I have shot him—what do I do with my litany? It doesn't disappear from my mind merely because there is no marauder anymore. Will I adopt it as a permanent creed?

I meet a young woman at a quiet dinner party, and as we sit together she tells me that she sometimes likes to go out with gangsters. She describes in detail the techniques they use in getting other people to do what they want—threats, bribery, violence. I'm shocked and repelled by the stories she tells. A few months later, I run into her again at another party, and I hear more stories, and for whatever reason I don't feel shocked. I'm no longer so aware of the sufferings of those whom the gangsters confront. I'm more impressed by the high style and shrewdness of the gangsters themselves. I begin to understand how difficult it is to be a successful gangster and what extraordinary skill is in fact required to climb to the top of a gangster empire. I find myself listening with a certain enjoyment. By the third time that I encounter this woman I've become a connoisseur of gangster techniques, and the stories she tells now strike me as funny. I consider myself to be, as I always was, a person who entirely disapproves of gangsters, but I still pass on to a friend of mine some of the best stories in the spirit of fun. If my friend now objects that the stories are not really funny, will I find myself somewhat annoyed? Will my friend now seem to me narrow-minded—a humorless bore?

And so every day we encounter the numberless insidious

intellectual ploys by which the principle of immorality makes a plausible case for itself, and for every ploy there is a corresponding weakness in our own thinking that causes us not to notice where we're being led until we've already fallen into the trap. Unfortunately, these small intellectual infirmities of ours—our brief lapses of concentration, our susceptibility to slightly inappropriate analogies, the way we tend to forget in what particular contexts the ideas in our heads first made their appearance there, the way our attention can be drawn at the wrong moment by the magician's patter to the hand that does not contain the mysterious coin—just happen to have the power to send history racing off down a path of horror. Morality, if it survived, could protect us from horror, but very little protects morality. And morality, besides, is hard to protect, because morality is only a few thoughts inside our heads. And just as we quickly grow accustomed to brutal deeds and make way before them, so we are quickly stunned into foggy submission by the brutal thoughts which, in our striving for comfort, we have allowed into our minds. And all the time we are operating under the illusion that we, mere individuals, have no power at all over the course of history, when that is in fact (for better or worse) the very opposite of the case.

The shocking truth is that history, too, is at the mercy of my thoughts, and the political leaders of the world sit by their radios waiting to hear whether morality has sickened or died inside my skull. The process is simple. I speak with you, and then I turn out the light, and I go to sleep, but, while I sleep, you talk on the telephone to a man you met last year in Ohio, and you tell him what I said, and then he calls up a neighbor of his, and what I said keeps traveling, farther and farther. And just as a fly can quite blithely and indifferently land on the nose of a queen, so the thought that you mentioned to the man in Ohio can make its way with unimaginable speed into the mind of a president. Because a society, among other things, is a network of brains, and a president is no less involved in his society's network than anyone else, and there is almost nothing that he thinks that doesn't come right from that network. In fact, he is virtually incapable of coming up with an attitude to any problem or to any event that has not been nurtured and developed in that network of brains. When it sooner or later becomes necessary for any of us, whether president or ordinary citizen, to come up with thoughts about political affairs, the only raw materials that we have to draw on are the thoughts we've previously formed—many of them simply thoughts about the conflicts and dramas of our daily lives. Our thoughts may be ones we've acquired from our parents, from our lovers, or from the man in Ohio. But wherever we've found them, they are all we have to work with. Our political attitudes can only come out of what we are—what we learned in school, at the playground, at the office, on the streets, at the party, at the beach, at the dinner table, in bed. And as all of our attitudes flow into action, flow into history, the bedroom and the battlefield soon seem to be one.

My political opinions fly out across the world and determine the course of political events. And political events are determined as well by what I think about the conversation I had with my mother last Saturday when we were having tea. What I say to you about my neighbor's child affects what you feel about the nurse who sits by the side of your friend in the hospital room, and what you say about the nurse affects what your friend's sister thinks about the government of Australia. Everything you are affects me, and everything I am, all my thoughts—the behavior I admire or criticize, the way I choose to spend an hour of my time, the things I like to talk about, the stories I like to hear, the jokes I like to tell—affect the course of history whether I like it or not, whether I know about it or not, whether I care or not. My power over history is inescapable except through death. Privacy is an illusion. What I do is public, and what I think is public. The fragility of my own thoughts becomes the fragility of the world. The ease with which I could become a swine is the ease with which the world could fall apart, like something rotten.

The uncomfortable and incompetent slaves of morality—those awkward, crippled creatures who insist on believing in a standard that condemns them—are less admirable only than those few perfect beings who perhaps obey morality completely. Yes, of course, if we have any sympathy or any affection for people—if we like people—we will be fond of many who treat morality indifferently. But this should not be allowed to confuse us. Morality happens to be a protection that we need in order to avoid total historical disaster, and so, unfortunately, we can't afford to turn our eyes away when our acquaintances, our friends, or we ourselves, drop down a few degrees on the scale of obedience to moral principles. It's obviously foolish and absurd to judge some small decline on the moral scale as if it were a precipitous, lengthy slide, but the temptation is great to be easy on ourselves, and we've all discovered that it's easier to be easy on ourselves if we're all easy on each other too, and so we are. So when a precipitous slide really does take place, a particular effort is required in order to see it. Sophistries, false chains of reasoning, deception, and self-deception all rush in to conceal the fact that any change has occurred at all.

If we live from day to day without self-examination, we remain unaware of the dangers we may pose to ourselves and the world. But if we look into the mirror, we just might observe a rapacious face. Perhaps the face will even show subtle traces, here and there, of viciousness and free-floating hate beneath the surface. All right then, we may say in response to the mirror, we are vile, we know it. Everyone is. That's the way people are.

This self-pitying response to the unflattering news that we're not quite good means that we've decided, if that's how things are, that we'll accept immorality, and we'll no longer make any effort to oppose it.

But it's utterly ridiculous to say that people are vile. If we step outside and pay a brief visit to the nearest supermarket or the nearest café, we'll find ourselves in a position to see, scattered perhaps among scenes of ugliness and greed, examples of behavior that is thoughtful or kind, moments when someone could easily have been cold or cruel but in fact was not. Perhaps we will see the very same person do something harsh and a moment later something gentle. Everyone knows that this element of goodness exists, that it can grow, or that it can die, and there's something particularly disingenuous about extricating oneself from the human struggle with the whispered excuse that it's already over.

Interview with Mark Strand
1998

The American poet Mark Strand says that the elements he requires in order to be able to write are "a place, a desk, a familiar room. I need some of my books there. I need quiet. That's about it." Asked if he ever writes in a less tranquil spot, such as on a train, he replies that he does, but usually only prose, because it's "less embarrassing. Who would understand a man of my age writing reams of poetry on a train, if they looked over my shoulder? I would be perceived as an overly emotional person."

Wallace Shawn: I started reading that thing that that guy wrote about you. But it upset me, because he kept talking about the themes of your writing, and I didn't get it. I don't think I really get the concept of "themes." So I'm not going to ask you questions like, What is your view of nothingness? because I don't get that, exactly.

Mark Strand: I don't get it either. And I'm not sure I could articulate a view of nothingness, since nothingness doesn't allow a description of itself. Once you start describing nothingness, you end up with somethingness.

WS: In any case, do we read poetry because we're interested in "themes"?

MS: You don't read poetry for the kind of truth that passes for truth in the workaday world. You don't read a poem to find out how to get to Twenty-fourth Street. You don't read a poem to find the meaning of life. The opposite. I mean, you'd be foolish to. Now, some American poets present the reader with a slice of life, saying, "I went to the store today, and I saw a man, and he looked at me, and I looked at him, and we both knew we were . . . thieves. And aren't we all thieves?" You know, this is extracting from everyday experience a statement about life, or a moral. But there is another type of poetry, in which the poet provides the reader with a surrogate world through which he reads *this* world. Wallace Stevens was the twentieth-century master of this. There's no other poetry that *sounds* like a Wallace Stevens poem. But then, there's nothing that sounds like a Frost poem, either. Or a Hardy poem. These people have created worlds of their own. Their language is so forceful and identifiable that you read them not to verify the meaning or truthfulness of your own experience of the world, but simply because you want to saturate yourself with their particular voices.

WS: Well, your poetry is obviously very much in this category. When we read your poetry, we are enticed by the voice—and then led into a world that you have created. And at first, I would say, we can more or less picture or imagine the scenes you conjure up, although they may consist of elements that in our daily world would never be combined in the way you've combined them. Sometimes, though, in your poems—quite often, really—we reach a point that is almost, one could say, Zeno-like, in which we're asked to imagine things that are either almost self-contradictory or literally unimaginable. I mean, in a surrealist painting, a painter could present a very strange landscape, but he couldn't present one like this! This couldn't be painted!

MS: Well, I think what happens at certain points in my poems is that language takes over, and I follow it. It just sounds right. And I trust the implication of what I'm saying, even though I'm not absolutely sure what it is that I'm saying. I'm just willing to let it be. Because if I were absolutely sure of whatever it was that I said in my poems, if I were sure, and could verify it and check it out and feel, yes, I've said what I intended, I don't think the poem would be smarter than I am. I think the poem would be, finally, a reducible item. It's this "beyondness," that depth that you reach in a poem, that keeps you returning to it. And you wonder—the poem seemed so natural at the beginning—how did you get where you ended up? What happened? I mean, I like that, I like it in other people's poems when it happens. I like to be mystified. Because it's really that place which is unreachable, or mysterious, at which the poem becomes ours, finally, becomes the possession of the reader. I mean, in the act of figuring it out, of pursuing meaning, the reader is absorbing the poem, even though there's an *absence* in the poem. But he just has to live with that. And eventually, it becomes essential that it exists in the poem, so that something beyond his understanding, or beyond his experience, or something that doesn't quite match up with his experience, becomes more and more his. He comes into possession of a mystery, you know—which is something that we don't allow ourselves in our lives.

WS: We don't?

MS: I mean, we live with mystery, but we don't like the feeling. I think we should get used to it. We feel we have to know what things mean, to be on top of this and that. I don't think it's human, you know, to be that competent at life. That attitude is far from poetry.

WS: An experience of total immersion in mystery that I once had was reading the first half of Heidegger's *Being and Time*. You know, it was really totally up to you to sort of create this world in your own head, and whether what was in your head was what was in Heidegger's head—who could possibly guess?

MS: Well, when I read poetry I can't imagine that what's in the reader's head is ever what was in the poet's head, because there's usually very little in the poet's head.

WS: You mean . . .

MS: I mean, I think the reality of the poem is a very ghostly one. It doesn't try for the kind of concreteness that fiction tries for. It doesn't ask you to imagine a place in detail; it suggests, it suggests, it suggests again. I mean, as *I* write it. William Carlos Williams had other ideas.

WS: But do you suggest something that you yourself have already pictured?

MS: I'm picturing it as I'm writing it. I'm putting together what I need in order to have this thing be alive. But sometimes it's more complete than at other times.

WS: When you say that when you write, language takes over, and then you follow it, you're implying that the experience of writing is one in which, at least to some extent, you're in a passive role. Something is coming to you from somewhere, and you're receiving it. But where is it coming from? Is it *just* the unconscious?

MS: Poems aren't dreams. They just aren't. It's something else. People who write down their dreams and think they're poems are wrong. They're neither dreams nor poems.

WS: But the type of poetry you're describing can be frustrating to the reader. A lot of people I know would have to admit that their basic model for reading would be something like the experience of reading the newspaper. Each sentence is supposed to match up to a particular slice of reality.

MS: If you want a poem to say what it means, right away, clearly—well, what happens when you read that kind of poem is that it puts you back in the world that you know. The poem makes that world seem a little more comfortable, because here is somebody else who has had an experience like yours. But you see, these little anecdotes that we read in these poems and that we like to believe are true, are in fact fictions. They represent a reduction of the real world. There's so much in our experience that we take for granted—we don't need to read poems that help us to take those things even *more* for granted. People like John Ashbery or Stevens do just the opposite—they try to explode those reductions. There's a desire in Ashbery, for example, to create perfect non sequiturs, to continually take us off guard. He creates a world that is fractured. But, looking at it from another point of view, you *could* say that it's simply a world that is as fractured and as unpredictable as the world in which we move every day. So there's an element of delight in these people who rearrange reality. We usually hang on to the predictability of our experiences to such an extent . . . and there's nowhere else where one can escape that as thoroughly as one can in certain poets' work. When I read poetry, I want to feel myself suddenly larger . . . in touch with—or at least close to—what I deem magical, astonishing. I want to experience a kind of wonderment. And when you report back to your own daily world after experiencing the strangeness of a world sort of recombined and reordered in the depths of a poet's soul, the world looks fresher somehow. Your daily world has been taken out of context. It has the voice of the poet written all over it, for one thing, but it also seems suddenly more alive—not as routinely there.

WS: Of course, when you talk about poetry in that way, you're going on the assumption that your reader is willing to put quite a bit of effort into following you—in contrast to writing for the theatre, for example, where it's more normal for one's colleagues to say, "The people aren't going to get this. Clarify it."

MS: I think a poet writes a poem not feeling that he must be understood on the first or second reading. He writes a poem hoping that the poem will be read more than once or twice, and its meaning will be revealed over the course of time, or its meaning will reveal itself over the course of time.

WS: When you say you hope that a poem will be read more than once or twice, how many times do you mean? How many times do *you* read a poem?

MS: When I write my own poems, I read them hundreds of times to myself. But when I read other people's poems I will read them dozens of times, sometimes more than dozens of times. I don't know why this should seem strange. The average church-going person who lives in the Bible Belt will have read the same passages in the Bible hundreds of times, and they will have revealed to him more each time.

WS: An actor in a play goes through a similar process, really, and acting could in a sense be seen as a form of reading, I suppose. The actor goes over the text hundreds of times, seeing more and more implications and different possible meanings inside each individual line, and at the same time seeing through the various clichés of interpretation with which he has at first mistakenly overlaid each line.

MS: Well, a good reader of poetry may be very much like an actor working on his part, because he reads the poem aloud to himself again and again, and sometimes he learns it by heart. And it becomes familiar. It, finally, becomes part of him. A poem releases itself, secretes itself, slowly—almost, sometimes, poisonously—into the mind of the reader. It does it with cadence, it does it with combinations that might strike the reader as beautiful. Of course, God knows what the beautiful is. I don't know. Because the beautiful fifty years from now will be what is seen as the ugly now or what's insupportable now or barely tolerated now. But, you know, I think if you try too hard to be immediately comprehensible to your audience, if you give too much to the moment, you're also giving too much to the status quo. The poet's obligation isn't to his audience, primarily, but to the language that he hopes he's perpetuating. And when you think of how long it takes us to understand each other, for example—and how much leeway we give other areas of knowledge in our lives—why can't we be a little more patient with poetry? The language of a poem is meant to be meditated on. You clear a psychic space for poetry. It's a space in which words loom large.

WS: But how does a person prepare such a psychic space?

MS: Well, if you spend a lot of time alone, particularly if you're thinking about your life, or other people's lives, you're already used to the space I'm talking about. There are certain painters I know to whom the language of poetry means a great deal. And it may be because these people spend a lot of time in front of canvases, alone, with nobody to talk to, that they're prepared: they're ready to take the poem in. Their minds are not full of a lot of noise and clutter and unfulfilled desire. I mean, you have to be willing to *read* poetry; you have to be willing to meet it halfway—because it won't go any further than that if it's any good. A poem has its dignity, after all. I mean, a poem shouldn't beg you to read it; it's pathetic, if that's the case. Some poets fear that they won't be heard unless they flatter the reader, go 90 percent of the way, do it all for the reader. But that's pathetic.

WS: Damn! I'm sort of worried that we're not living in the right world to read what you and the poets you admire are writing.

MS: Well, poetry—at least lyric poetry—tries to lead us to relocate ourselves in the self. But everything we want to do these days is an escape from self. People don't want to sit home and think. They want to sit home and watch television. Or they want to go out and have fun. And having fun is not usually meditative. It doesn't have anything to do with reassessing one's experience and finding out who one is or who the other guy is. It has to do with burning energy. When you go to the movies, you're overcome with special effects and monstrous goings-on. Things unfold with a rapidity that's thrilling. You're not given a second to contemplate the previous scene, to meditate on something that's just happened. Something else takes its place. We forget that there is a thrill that attends the slower pleasures, pleasures that become increasingly powerful the more time we spend pursuing them.

WS: Maybe language in general is slowly losing out in some sort of weird competition in the world.

MS: Well, but on the other hand, we do talk to one another. We would be lonely if we didn't use words.

WS: Maybe people avoid poetry because it somehow actively makes them nervous or anxious.

MS: They don't want to feel the proximity of the unknown—or the mysterious. It's too deathlike; it's too threatening. It suggests the possibility of loss of control right around the corner.

WS: When you say deathlike . . .

MS: Well, when I say the unknown—death is the great unknown. I mean, most lyric poems lead to some acknowledgment of death. In fact, most poems are dark and dreary affairs that have to do with death and dying, or loss of one sort or another—loss of love, loss of friends, loss of life. Most lyric poems are sad, because if you think deeply at all about your experience, you think about your experience in time—your life—and if you're thinking about your life, you can't avoid the fact that it will end in death. In fact, everything about a poem—the meter of the poem, or the measure of the poem—is a reminder of time. Even a line that's repeated: we're back again. I think that the popularity of villanelles or poems that use refrains is caused by the fact that they seem to enact a stay against time, they seem to give us a momentary reprieve from what usually is the subject of the poem, or the matter of the poem. So, although the poem may be about dying or death, we have repeated lines that seem to say we haven't really gone anywhere, we're back again. But in the end, that just helps us to hold on to the loss that is in the poem. It helps us to remember it.

WS: In some of your own poems, death is kind of disturbing, but in others, it isn't that bad . . . But if poetry in a way is inherently disturbing and likely to provoke anxiety, is prose any different?

MS: Well, I think a poet's focus is not quite what a prose writer's is; it's not entirely on the world outside. It's fixed on that area where the inside meets the outside, where the poet's sensibility meets the weather, meets the street, meets other people, meets what he reads. So a poet describes that point of contact: the self, the edge of the self, and the edge of the world. That shadow land between self and reality. Sometimes the focus is tipped slightly in favor of the self, sometimes, more objectively, in favor of the world. And so sometimes, when the balance is tipped toward the self, strange things are said, odd things get into the poem. Because the farther you are from the world that everybody recognizes as the world, the stranger things look. I mean, some novels do this, but most don't. There are some narrators who insert themselves, as Philip Roth does brilliantly and amazingly. I'm always dazzled by his books. The world is electrically alive in *American Pastoral*, for example, but he's there, too: Roth is Zuckerman, and he's there, he's telling the story. In a sense, that book is more magical than any poem I've read recently.

WS: I had no idea you were such a Philip Roth fan. So am I! Do you think of yourself as someone who reads widely in many different sorts of books? Would you call yourself a person who spends a lot of time reading?

MS: I have gone through periods in my life of reading a great deal, and others in which I barely touched a book. There are certain novels I enjoy reading and rereading. There are poets I read and reread. There was a period at one time when I read Wittgenstein. There was a period when I read the romantic poets, and would read Wordsworth quite a lot. There was never a period in my adult life when I didn't read and reread Wallace Stevens, or Elizabeth Bishop. There's never been a period in my adult life when I haven't derived pleasure from reading Philip Roth or, on the other hand, Samuel Beckett. Or Italo Calvino, or Tommaso Landolfi. Or Bruno Schulz, or Franz Kafka. Great poets like Octavio Paz I've read and reread over the years, Joseph Brodsky, Derek Walcott. There are also younger poets I read with a sense of awe: Jorie Graham, Charles Wright, Charles Simic.

WS: What did you mean when you said that a poet's first responsibility was to the language?

MS: Well, in writing poetry, one wants a certain flexibility in the use of language, a flexibility that can keep alive successes in the language from the past, that is, other poems, and that will also ensure that whatever poetry comes next will capitalize on the successes instead of on the failures. The fact is that we take many of our cues on how to proceed, and our ideas about what is a good line, or a beautiful line, from what we've experienced from the poetry of the past. In other words, it would be nice to know that poets in the future will have read the best poets of today and yesterday, that they won't simply base their poems on news reports or instruction manuals. You know, so that there's some continuity in the language of poetry. Because it's complicated, but we're defined by the best that's written in our language, and so we want to perpetuate the best that's written in our language. If poetry becomes just a revision of the newspaper page or the talking heads on TV, that's not a language that will last; it's not a language that translates into the future.

WS: But then what would you think of a poet, or someone who said he was a poet, a student, let's say, who came to you and said, "Well, I'm only interested in the present. I don't know about the poetry of the past, I don't like it, and I'm not too interested in it?"

MS: Well, I would ask him, "What poetry have you read that makes you feel that you want to write poetry?" Because usually what draws us toward poetry is the individual voice that we want to hear—the voice of Wordsworth, the voice of Keats, James Merrill, Anthony Hecht, whoever it is. The chances are that a person who doesn't feel any desire to hear such voices may not turn out to have a very original voice himself.

WS: So you do in a way agree with the academic writers who always seem to imply that the parents of poems are other poems, as opposed to what I'm always wondering, which is why couldn't the greatest influences on a poet be the people he's known, or the experiences he's had every day, rather than the poems he's read?

MS: Well, it all depends on the poetry you write. Some people may be more influenced by their mothers and less influenced by Robert Frost. It differs with different poets. But by and large, I think poets are more influenced by other poems than they are by what they eat and whom they talk to—because they read other poems deeply, and sometimes they don't eat dinner deeply or chat with a friend over the telephone deeply. Because poems not only demand patience, they demand a kind of surrender. You must give yourself up to them. Once you've done that, and allowed them to enter into your system, of course they're going to be more influential. This is the real food for a poet: other poems, not meatloaf.

WS: But what about the idea that a poet should be influenced by a wide range of experience, that a poet should explore *life* and allow it to affect him? Don't you have any feeling that you should do everything, at least once?

MS: I don't have to try everything on the menu to know what it is that I like. I can make a reasonable guess as to what I *might* like, and so that's what I will order. I don't go out of my way to experience every possible thing, because that's dangerous. I want to protect myself. I want not to experience many, many different things, but to experience the things I choose to experience well, and deeply.

WS: Some writers, for example, have tried to enhance their work by writing under the influence of alcohol or drugs.

MS: They interfere. I mean, if I've had a couple of drinks, I don't feel like writing. I feel like having another drink. Or I feel like going to sleep.

WS: But if poems, including poems from the past, are really a poet's main food, doesn't that lead to some rather odd consequences? For example, poets always seem to love to quote other poems in their poetry. I mean—my God—if a contemporary playwright put lines from some nineteenth-century play in one of his own plays, it would be considered, well, ludicrously academic.

MS: Well, too much of that can be burdensome or overbearing. But sometimes it's delightful; sometimes there's a perfect line that just fits in your poem, and it comes from a poem that's a hundred years old. Poetry is always building these connections. It's not showing off. It's the verbalization of the internal life of man. And each poet forges a link in the chain, so that it can go on. That may be a grandiose way to think of it, but it's certainly not academic. I mean, academics really know very little about poetry; they experience it from the outside. Some of them are ideal readers, but their job is to make connections. It's the way they read, the way they have to read. But why should we allow the reading of an academic to become a paradigm for the way we *all* should read?

WS: Well, but some modern poetry, like *The Waste Land*, has been so full of connections—connections and allusions—that emergency academic help has been required in order to read it.

MS: Yes, it would have been impossible for me to have read *The Waste Land* without critical intervention.

WS: But isn't there something wrong with that? Or don't you think so? I mean, you don't write like that.

MS: No.

WS: Well, why don't you? Would you write that way if you felt like it—or do you have any objection to that?

MS: I don't. I mean, Eliot was a very learned guy and, you know—he wrote a very allusive poetry. My poetry is much more self-contained. I think that there are all kinds of poetry possible—there are all kinds of people possible. *The Waste Land*, the *Cantos* of Pound—this is one kind of poetry. It's a very extreme case of allusiveness. These are men who were intent on revising culture; that found its way into their poetry.

WS: And you're willing to make that journey?

MS: Sure!

WS: It's worth it? You don't think it's an outrageous thing to do?

MS: No. By what standard would it be outrageous? Only by the standard of how easily one can understand the daily newspaper. But say one's standard were trying to understand what is most difficult and most elusive in ourselves. How do we know who we are, and what we are? How do we know why we said what we said? If you use that as a standard, then *The Waste Land* becomes simple. Well, less difficult.

WS: The problem is that, because of the existence of very allusive modern poetry, a lot of people, at least in my generation, were given in their school days a sort of screwy idea of what poetry *is*, and it put them off poetry for life. I'm very grateful that I had some wonderful English teachers, because the bad ones did try to teach us that poetry was simply a game, in which you substituted a certain group of words for the code words offered by the poet. When the poet said *water*, you crossed it out and wrote *rebirth*, et cetera. It was all, "This is a symbol of this, this is a symbol of that." And in a certain way, we got to *hate* those symbols.

MS: Well, rightfully. It sounds tyrannical on the part of the teacher to submit you, and to submit the poem, to that. I mean, I don't think teachers who are forced to teach poetry know why they're teaching it, or what poetry provides. Some poems aren't paraphrasable, just as some experiences can't be readily understood—and yet we live with those experiences. I mean, we can love a poem and not understand it, I think. There's no reason why we can't live with a poem that doesn't deliver meaning right away—or perhaps ever. You know, somebody should have asked the teacher, "What's the relationship between the meaning of a poem and the *experience* of a poem?"

WS: We didn't have an experience!

MS: It's as if the paraphrase of the poem was meant to take the place of the poem, and the poem was lost.

WS: I'm afraid so.

MS: You know, the idea is to experience the poem! But this

is the reversal that takes place: the poem becomes a surrogate for what the teacher has to say about it.

WS: Well, I mean, *literally*, because in my old schoolbooks, the physical poem is actually obliterated by the notes I've taken on the teacher's interpretations. The page is a swirl of arrows and circles and scrawled-in words. You could never read the original poem.

MS: I don't know why teachers are afraid of the *experience* of the poem . . .

WS: Well, because it would be like passing out drugs in class, I imagine.

MS: Poetry *is* a high. It is a thrill. If people were taught to read poetry in the right way, they would find it extremely pleasurable.

WS: It's also an experience of close contact with another mind, another person.

MS: Well, certainly something I would want a reader to have as he experiences my poetry is—a form of intimacy.

WS: Yes. But of course—how can I put this—as a reader, I wouldn't want to have that intimacy with everybody.

MS: No. You have to like the voice. I mean, you have to like the music you hear.

WS: Right. And it's quite a personal and individual matter what voices you like. It's hard to predict. Like a lot of our other most personal preferences, it goes deep into the individual psyche.

MS: Well, I feel that anything is possible in a poem. But the problem is, as a poet develops, he develops a predisposition to use certain words—which create or suggest certain landscapes, or interiors, or certain attitudes. Those, in fact, become his identity as a poet. So when a subject with a vocabulary he has never used asserts itself, it may be difficult to accommodate. It will seem strange and may eventually be repudiated in favor of the words that he or she knows will work, because finally—despite experimentation and all the self-righteousness attendant on experimentation—it's more of our own poems that we want to write, more of *our own poems*, poems that sound like they were written by us. It's a terrible limitation. I mean, in some ways, this is where John Ashbery's genius is so marked—that he's got such a large vocabulary that it accommodates everything. He can talk about Goebbels, or hummingbirds, steam shovels and hemorrhoids, all in the same poem. And he could do it, probably, within ten lines and it would sound like Ashbery!

WS: Allen Ginsberg once implied that he wrote "Howl" in one draft, without revising it, although later he said he actually did revise it a lot. Have you ever been interested in trying the no-revision approach?

MS: Well, I would *like* to write just one draft of a poem and have done with it, but it rarely happens. It's only happened a very few times. You know, I'm not one of the geniuses that gets it right the first time. But there are people who do.

WS: Well, there *may* be. We'll never know—they may secretly be hiding a thousand drafts of their poems. Anyway, who cares? If we read something and we like it, we don't care whether it took someone a long time or a short time to write it.

MS: I don't think the writer should care. We're lucky to write a few terrific things in our lifetime, and for all we know, we may already have written them. So, who knows? I know nothing of the value of my work—all I know is that it's what I do, and what I love to do.

WS: Did you feel differently when you were thirty? Because I did.

MS: Oh, I felt very differently. I was much more ambitious. I felt that I was destined to hold a special place. That's what I needed in those days to keep me writing. I don't need that anymore, and I don't believe any of that obtains. But if young writers talk to me in those terms, I understand very well what they mean, and I'm sympathetic.

WS: But all the same, doesn't it sometimes bother you that millions of people don't revere you? I mean, don't you sometimes feel that you ought to be honored for your accomplishments everywhere you go? After all, you *deserve* it.

MS: Well, some people like my poetry a great deal. It's better than *nobody* liking it.

WS: But what about the millions of other people?

MS: There are a few people I know whose feeling about my poetry is the most important thing to me. It's as simple as that. I don't know many of the people who read my poems. I don't even know, when they read my poems, whether they like my poems. There's no way for me to know, so I can't worry about it.

WS: Yes, but all the same, don't you sometimes resent the fact that certain other people in our culture are so incredibly idolized? For example, I was recently listening to a CD of Elliott Carter, and I was thinking, Isn't it unbelievable that this man, who has created such incredibly subtle and beautiful music, is much less honored in our society than people who write songs using only three or four chords? Doesn't he have a reason to be outraged about that?

MS: Well, the people who like those three or four chords probably aren't going to like his music.

WS: No.

MS: And he probably wouldn't want to be popular with that set.

MS: No, he wouldn't.

MS: So there's no complaint.

WS: You mean, these are two different audiences. So that would be like playing elephant music to giraffes.

MS: There is only one reason to be envious of the people who write very successful songs with three or four chords, and that is that they earn the kind of money that gives them a kind of freedom that Elliott Carter may not have. So it would be nice for Elliott Carter to go to the restaurants that Elton John can afford.

But if the price was that he had to write music exactly like Elton John's, then he would do without it. And that's it. If I had to write the kind of sentences that Jacqueline Susann wrote, you know, write the kind of novels that she wrote, I wouldn't be able to hold my head high anywhere! I'd *slink* into restaurants—very expensive restaurants—and I'd *slink* into expensive hotels. And I'd be ashamed to say what it was that I did.

WS: But don't you find it sort of awful that our society doesn't even respect poetry enough to allow poets to support themselves through their writing?

MS: I think poetry would be different if people could make a living writing poetry. Then you would have to satisfy certain expectations. Instead of the inherited norms by which we recognize poems to be poems, there would be a whole new set of constraints, and not such enduring ones, having to do with the marketplace, having to do with what sells, or what engages people in the short run. So perhaps poetry is better off having no monetary value.

WS: If I may speak of you personally, it seems that, for better or worse, writing poetry is an essential part of your identity, your sense of yourself—am I right about that?

MS: Well, my identity is hopelessly wrapped up in what I write, and my being a writer. If I stopped writing, I would simply feel the loss of myself. When I don't write, I don't feel properly alive. There was a period in my life, for five years, when I didn't write any poems. They were among the saddest years of my life, perhaps the saddest years. I wrote a lot of other things. None of them satisfied me the way the writing of poetry does, but I did them, just because I had to be ready, in case poetry came back into my life and I felt capable enough to write poems that weren't terrible. I refuse to write if I feel the poems I'm writing are bad. My identity is not that important, finally. Not dishonoring what I consider a noble craft is more important. I would rather not write than write badly and dishonor poetry—

even if it meant I wasn't properly myself. I mean, this sounds high and noble, but in fact, it's not. I love poetry. I love myself, but I think I love poetry as much as I love myself.

WS: You don't seem to share the attitude that some people have of, "Hey, I enjoy my hedonistic life of reading and writing, and I don't have the faintest idea whether what I do benefits society or not, and I couldn't care less."

MS: No. That's not my thing at all. I'm *certain* that what I do, and what other poets do, is important.

WS: I have to ask you one more personal question. Well, I don't have to, but I will, because I'm curious: Do you care whether you're read after you're dead?

MS: Well, not to be funny about this, but I'm sort of split on the issue. I mean, I would like to be read after I'm dead, but that's projection.

WS: You mean, because you're imagining . . . ?

MS: I mean, I'd really like to be *alive* after I'm dead. That's all that is. I don't really think it will make much difference to me when I'm dead whether I'm read or not.

WS: Right.

MS: Just as whether I'm *dead* or not won't mean much to me when I'm dead. You see?

WS: Sure. So the issue of whether your work is read after your death . . .

MS: I think most people who have published books, whose career is a matter of public record, will be read for a little while and then dropped. I mean, after a while, almost everybody is dropped to make room for the new. I think that's only fair. I just hope that the new, or the next, includes poetry. That's what I want. Poetry must continue.

Breakfast Table with Jewish Newsletters
2021

Jewish.

I'm Jewish.

Excuse me? Are you talking about me?

Excuse me, but I think "I" am the consciousness I woke up with this morning. And I think that's more or less the consciousness I wake up with every day and have woken up with every day since my birth. Right? And my consciousness has no race.

Now. I'm associated with my body. Somehow. But it's complicated. Very complicated. When I walk down the street and I catch sight of "myself" in the mirror of a shop window, I ask, "Who's that?" and I answer, "Oh yes. It's that guy again."

But that guy has been assigned to me. There's a connection there. He's connected to me. He's "my" body. If you hit him, I suffer. If you caress him, I'm comforted. If you torture him, he almost becomes me—almost—there's not much me left beyond the pain that he feels. And if you kill him, I'm gone. But all the same, he's a body, and I'm not. He's not me.

And yes, my body has a certain history behind it. It is what it is because of its genes. It made itself, bit by bit, following the instructions of its genes. And the genes gave their instructions according to some very strict laws. So—where did the genes come from, I wonder? Did they come from Israel? Is my body Jewish? Did my genes come from some people who called themselves "Jews?"

Well—as there were no people at all who called themselves "Jews" before around 3300 B.C., obviously my genes don't come from them entirely. Before about 3300 B.C., there were no Jews, but there were other humans, called different things, or called nothing, and the genes of the Jews came from them. The Jews did not invent their own genes. The Jews inherited their genes from their ancestors, who, like everybody else's ancestors, were descendants of the early humans, our original ancestors, who lived in Africa. Most of my genes are direct copies of the genes of the African ancestors. But of course the African ancestors got most of their genes from proto-humans and various primates and early mammals and early fish-like creatures.

So, if you like, you can say that my genes came from various people, some Jewish and some not—or you could say that they came from cells, from egg cells and sperm cells, cells that had developed in certain human bodies, without, interestingly, any intervention of the people, the personalities, associated with those bodies. In other words, the genes didn't know whose body they were in, and the people who carried those genes didn't know where their genes came from or how they got there.

I was sitting at my breakfast table, and it was November 25, 2020, six months to the day since George Floyd, an African-American father of five, had been asphyxiated on a public street by Derek Chauvin, a Minneapolis policeman. I'd finished my breakfast, and I was reading two things at the same time. To one side of me, there was a cereal box with writing on it, and to the other side of me there was my open computer. The cereal box, in bold letters, proudly declared that the cereal inside it was "Made From American Corn." And the computer was open to the morning's email and specifically to one of the many newsletters I seem to receive every morning from different Jewish organizations to which I'd never belonged. The killing of George Floyd and the extraordinary response it provoked had made me—and probably almost everyone in the United States—hyper-conscious of the issue of "race," and so on this particular morning I was wondering idly whether the daily appearance of these newsletters meant that my name was somewhere inscribed on some list of people who'd been determined to be members of the Jewish "race." And at the same time, I was wondering about the cereal box and inevitably asking myself, Well, can corn really be "American?" Yes, the corn used in the cereal in the box may be grown in America, but can an ear of corn actually be American? Can it be American even though it doesn't know that it is? The ear of corn has a complicated ancestry going back to the origin of life in the primeval ocean. And rather than saying that it's associated with America, couldn't you just as well say that it's associated with the primeval ocean? And of course my body also has a complex ancestry. For example, along with asking, Is my body associated with people who called themselves Jews? one might possibly ask, Is my body not equally associated with those remarkable fish who figured out how to survive on land? And I might also ask, If I say that I'm Jewish, does that mean, for example, that my liver is Jewish? What if some of the particular genes that served as the blueprint for my liver came from ancestors who didn't call themselves Jews? Would I then have an alien non-Jewish liver in a Jewish body?

If a dog is born in America, is the dog American?

Or is my body African? Am I African?

If a horse is born inside the state of Israel, is the horse Jewish?

The subject of these Jewish newsletters is, first and foremost, anti-Semitism. Not for the most part the horrible murders of Jews that have occurred in the last few years in Europe and the United States, or the desecrations of Jewish cemeteries or the swastikas written on walls—most of the newsletters have devoted much more space to hinting or outright declaring that certain individuals, including various American and British politicians, are anti-Semitic.

We live in a world obsessed by race, a world in which people are killed again and again because of race. But what is "race," exactly?

The idea of "race" itself first became popular in the eighteenth century, but humans learned how to categorize—and, specifically, how to categorize each other—long before the invention of "race." Individuals learned how to see themselves as belonging to a specific group, to formulate the thought that the people in their own group were very, very different from the people in other groups, and also to imagine that the people in other groups were inferior—bad, ugly, dangerous, disgusting, frightening, perhaps uncannily disturbing. And still, today, this ability to categorize, along with the ability to like and dislike, remain key to our functioning, and strangely these capacities operate independently of our will, in fact they operate in a part of our minds to which we don't have conscious access. That is, they live in the part of our minds that is hidden from our own awareness and that we ourselves had no role in creating. So if a dove happens to land on my windowsill, I feel happy, and I think, "Hello! I like you," but if a pigeon lands there, I feel slightly repelled, and I think, "Oh, I don't like you, can you please go away?" And why do I have these particular feelings? I have absolutely no idea. Whoever put those feelings inside me, it wasn't me.

The concept of "race" is based on the belief that humanity consists of a few distinct groups of humans that developed quite separately from each other in separate geographical areas. To put the belief in "race" into the language of genetics would be to claim that each of the groups or "races" is genetically distinct, so that the individuals in each race are genetically similar to each other and genetically dissimilar to individuals from other races. Those who believe in "race" believe that each particular race has certain infallibly defining physical markers, such as skin color and certain facial features. And of course some believers in "race" believe that the members of each race share distinct inherited moral attributes. Adolf Hitler's officials routinely measured different parts of people's bodies in order to determine whether or not those people were members of the

Jewish "race," and, if it was determined that they were, Hitler believed that they inevitably had inherited various despicable moral qualities and deserved to be killed, even if they were children or infants who hadn't had a chance to manifest many qualities at all.

There's never been any evidence that moral qualities can be found in our genes or that moral qualities could be inherited. Bodies, when born, have no beliefs, no customs, and no moral traits. And the study of human pre-history has revealed that, far from snuggling down in a few distinct geographical areas, as the "race" theory would have it, our particular variety of humans, possessed of a wild and dynamic restlessness, was constantly breaking up and splintering off into different groups, moving from one place to another, repeatedly crossing astonishing distances to reach distant continents, and because of the strange nature of sexual desire, and the frightening brutality of the human male, as these groups broke up into still other groups, some staying put in their old locations, others moving on, as they traveled, explored, sought to avoid starvation, sought to find a better life, plundered, fought, conquered, formed new communities, ran into other groups and sometimes joined them, as they intermarried and raped, their genes kept crazily jumping over every mountain, river, and desert. Some groups settled down long enough for genetic mutations to spread in the group, so that almost everyone in the group would have the same characteristic eyebrows, but somehow, a few thousand years later, people could be found with those very same eyebrows a few thousand miles away. By today, very few people on the planet, if any, have genes that come from only one group or only one geographical area. In any case, it turns out that people who belong to a particular "race," if that is defined by their skin color, facial features, or other measurable characteristics, may have fewer genes in common with members of "their own" "race" than they have with people who are not members of their "race" at all, so that, in other words, the whole idea of "race" is based on a series of misconceptions and refers to something that doesn't actually exist.

Nonetheless, for most of us today, the principal categorizing obsession continues to be categorization by race. Indeed, the idea of race remains so invincibly powerful that it floods the basement of our minds, the not-conscious part of our minds, and it influences our behavior when we're not aware of it, and it weaves itself through the semi-conscious thoughts that are our banal burden as we go through each day.

Bob walks into a room. Joe is already sitting there. Bob's grandmother came from China, and Bob spent many years of his childhood in China and was deeply influenced by Chinese culture. But the laws of genetics gave him his father's dark skin. So Joe thinks, "There's Bob. Bob's black." Joe thinks that he himself is "white," and Bob thinks that Joe is "white." Bob lives in a country in which most people are identified as "white," so Bob is less aware that Joe is "white" than Joe is aware that Bob is "black." The situation is potentially scary for Bob, and the country he lives in is a scary place for Bob, because Bob can be shot because people think he's "black." But Bob is not black. Bob has genes from all of his ancestors. Some of his ancestors were slaves. Some of them were slave-masters. And some of them were neither masters nor slaves. Some were Chinese. The laws of genetics gave Bob's skin the very specific color it has, which is not black, and the same laws gave Joe's skin the very specific color his has, which is not white.

Knowing the color of Bob's skin and the shape of his facial features tells you nothing about Bob as a human being. Knowing the color of Joe's skin and the shape of his facial features tells you nothing about Joe as a human being. But Bob and Joe can't escape the power of the "race" idea.

Bob and Joe are both professors. Joe is sitting in the faculty lounge. Bob and Joe have met a couple of times, but they don't know each other. Bob approaches Joe and says, "Hey, are they having that meeting tomorrow?" and Joe replies, "No, it's going to be Friday." But as Bob approaches him, Joe can't help thinking, "Here comes Bob. Bob is black. Black black black black black," even though he tries not to think it, and Bob, because he lives in a world in which most of the people he meets every day are people he thinks of as white, is not that surprised that Joe is someone he thinks of as white, but Bob is a rather worn-out guy, because he has a hundred encounters every day like this, and each is an effort. Bob and Joe both wish that their encounters could be relaxed, easy, un-worried, un-self-conscious, unconstrained, spontaneous, and effortless, that is, without an awareness of "race," without an awareness of the ways in which it's bad luck to be seen as "black" and good luck to be seen as "white," and without an awareness of the fact that Bob might possibly feel resentful towards people seen as "white," or Joe might possibly be afraid of people seen as "black" or feel guilty towards people seen as "black," or both, and they're both probably saying to themselves, "Don't think about all that." But we're rarely very successful when we tell ourselves "Don't think about X" or "Don't feel Y." And if I'm poor and you're rich, even though it might in certain circumstances be much better for both of us if we both forgot those facts, the problem is that if I remain poor, it's really only going to be a matter of time before I re-discover the situation and think, "Hey, you're rich."

Beyond "race," we continue our compulsive categorizing into smaller groups. In the United States, where I live, everyone boringly and pointlessly categorizes all day long by national background, along with race. Individuals with Spanish ancestry may have a skin color identical to someone with French ancestry, but those with French ancestry are called "white," while those with Spanish ancestry are called "non-white" or "Hispanic." And for each racial or national category, there are various corresponding stereotypes and prejudices.

A friend promised to give me a book, and he said that the book had been written by a man who was a physicist. When he gave me the book, I experienced a moment of surprise. I was surprised to see that the author had an Italian name. I simply hadn't expected that the physicist would be Italian. After a few micro-seconds, I recalled that many of the world's greatest scientists had been Italian and that there was no reason to be surprised that this physicist was Italian. But the moment of surprise revealed a not-conscious attitude. I wouldn't have been surprised if an opera singer had turned out to be Italian, but apparently I was surprised that a physicist had turned out to be Italian. If anyone had asked me if I'd been surprised to learn that the author of the book, the physicist, was Italian, I would certainly have denied it. And I would have denied it with a certain feeling of sincerity, as my conscious self was not surprised—not after the apparently meaningless initial moment of surprise. And it's not the sort of moment I would normally ever mention to anyone else or even remember or even explicitly admit to myself.

The not-conscious, the basement, happens to be the biggest room in most of our houses, and the stereotypes, the fears, and the beliefs about different groups that have been ladled like a sort of hideously unhealthy dishwater into that basement since our childhoods, have all become part of the vast oceanic chaos of our not-conscious minds, along with countless irrational taboos, the folklore about sex, the outlandish and inaccurate stories about people we know and don't know, the books we've read but no longer remember, the lessons from school about the weather and the solar system, the old comic books, the old television shows, and all the thoughts that have ever been expressed to us. It's very easy for thoughts to get into the basement of our minds, but because we don't have direct access to it, it's not so easy for us to reach into that basement and pull thoughts out, and this is true for all of us, no matter how enlightened or well-meaning or intelligent or sophisticated we may think that we are.

And in addition, the prejudices and stereotypes and other ludicrous ideas in our not-conscious basement minds are not even usually the most up-to-date ones. Personally, although born in the 1940's, I consider myself extremely hip and fully at home in the world of the 2020's where I live today, but if, looking at them objectively, my conscious thoughts are, on average, typical thoughts of the 1990's, my not-conscious thoughts are probably, on average, typical thoughts of the 1950's. And of course my conscious thoughts wrestle with my not-conscious thoughts every day. Sometimes they win, and sometimes they lose. But the not-conscious thoughts, when vanquished, don't evaporate. They simply hide in a deeper part of the basement, waiting for a day which I hope will never come, the day when the worst parts of me are somehow activated, and I become the dreadful person I know I'm capable of becoming.

And considering the very real problems that have always threatened us—hunger, ill health, starvation, and now the death of species, the rising temperatures, the rising seas—it's a fantastical and almost unbelievable fact that humanity has invented for itself a ridiculous and utterly unnecessary problem, racism. And it's mind-boggling as well that all over the world, and over the years, and most particularly today, grotesquely swaggering, bloated creatures called political "leaders" have actually convinced large numbers of people to love and revere them precisely by encouraging those who listen to them to drink deeper and deeper from the cup of racism. But to add to the depressing facts about this unnecessary invention, racism, we have to observe not only that racism is awful, but that many of the most natural responses to it are also awful.

Obviously, to speak of myself, although my genes came from countless different people, a lot of them were people who called themselves "Jews," and my parents and most of my relatives, with varying degrees of interest, commitment, or enthusiasm, thought of themselves as "Jews," and if by chance I walk into a room and catch the whiff of a lit cigar, I'm suffused with a sensation of warmth and coziness, because my Jewish grandfather and uncles smoked cigars, and in fact I've even felt at certain moments a twinge of pleasure and maybe almost of pride when someone has said something like, "Hey, did you know that Camille Pissarro was Jewish?" But basically for the most part I've thought all too little about my ancestry, and days and weeks go by without my thinking about whether I'm Jewish or not—or even thinking the word "Jewish" for any reason at all.

It's natural for every person to wonder every once in a while, "What am I?" And in my own life so far, I've thought about that subject every once in a while in the privacy of my own mind. But there are moments in history when other people—in recent centuries, racists—try to answer the question for us.

If I'd been born eighty or ninety years ago, anti-Semites would have defined me simply and without any hesitation as "a Jew" because of my ancestry and my facial features. And if because of being defined as a Jew, I'd lost my job, and I'd had to live in a ghetto, and I'd been forced to wear a yellow star on my clothing, and I'd been surrounded everywhere by people who showed contempt for me, and I'd been spat on in the street, and I'd been beaten up, and my aunts and uncles, my parents, my brothers and sisters, had been arrested or shot or seized at dawn and taken away to concentration camps—well, then, of course I would have been obsessed by my Jewishness. I would have thought about it every minute of every day because it would have dominated my life every minute of every day. I couldn't have ignored the subject of my "race," just as an African-American in the United States today can't possibly ignore the subject of their "race."

If a person has been defined by others as being a member of a disfavored group, and that group is being denigrated by everyone around them, they may respond by accepting the negative description of themselves, and they may become depressed and fall into a state of passivity, they may despise themselves and feel worthless, powerless, and weak. On the other hand, if people around them are speaking contemptuously about their group, they might possibly respond by wanting to honor their group. Or if others are trying to take away from them the styles of cooking, the songs, the games that they associate with their childhood, with their relatives, with their family, then they might feel motivated to appreciate and revere those cultural treasures. And if they and the people around them are subjected to a common assault, their response might be to identify with the threatened community. In fact, in certain circumstances of threat or danger, it wouldn't even be something a person would need to think about; the identification would be automatic and total.

The killing of Jews in Europe in very large numbers began in the twelfth century. The myth spread that Jews used the blood of Christian children in their rituals, and for this mythical crime, for example, thirty-eight Jews were burned at the stake in the small French town of Blois in 1171. And when the Black Plague spread across Europe in the fourteenth century, Jews were accused of causing the plague by poisoning the wells, and Jews were massacred all over Europe, and when they were not massacred, they were frequently expelled from the places where they'd lived. Eventually "the Jew" became a symbol for many Christians of all that was vile, even as fewer and fewer Christians had the opportunity to meet a Jew during the course of their lives. So these sorts of things have been going on for a very, very long time. Remarkably, also for a very, very long time, Jews have collected together with other Jews and attempted to preserve their beliefs, culture, and sense of community. Some Jews also tried in a sense to form a community with other Jews long dead, with all the Jews who had lived in the previous five thousand years.

The idea of preserving or fortifying a five-thousand-year-old

Jewish community persists today in various forms. In countries all over the world, there are Jews who pay respect to Jewish ancestors by celebrating Jewish holidays and observing Jewish customs. Some try to honor their Jewish heritage by attempting to live up to the extraordinary principles expressed in Jewish texts about justice and the good life. Others attend synagogues or practice the religion of Judaism. And still others center their lives around their participation in small enclosed societies made up exclusively of Jews. For some, the "we" of the five-thousand-year-old Jewish community is of much greater importance in their daily experience than is their own personal "I." These individuals teach their children to recite the prayers and practice the customs which they believe to be the same as the prayers and customs that their ancestors had recited and practiced, and they tell their children, using the powerful word "our," "These are our prayers and customs. These are our beliefs. These are the prayers and beliefs and customs that my parents handed down to me and that you will hand down to your own children." They believe that they share the same attitudes towards life as their ancient ancestors, and some even dress like Jews of medieval times. The identification can be so complete that they will use the word "we" without reservation or self-consciousness even when they tell their children—and encourage their children to tell their own future children—"We had a great kingdom, we were warriors, we were invincible, we were persecuted, we were slaves, we suffered, we were killed."

Of course if a person in the modern world tries to say things and do things that a Jew from medieval times might have said or done, that doesn't make them a Jew from medieval times. For a person to imitate an owl doesn't make them an owl. And the fact that a person is descended from a one-celled organism doesn't make them a one-celled organism. Just as the medieval pronunciation and the medieval context and associations of the words used in medieval prayers can be guessed at but not known, the attitudes towards life of medieval Jews can be guessed at but not known. And while children can be taught to think of themselves as part of a group, they are not actually born as members of a group. The European racists believed that a person's physical ancestry, the ancestry of their body, determined what sort of person they would be, and if they were born to Jewish parents, the racists believed they'd be terrible people. Some of the more devoted protectors of the five thousand-year-old Jewish community also believe in a destiny determined by ancestry, but they believe that if a person is born to Jewish parents, they're born Jewish, as if the customs, prayers, and beliefs were part of their physical inheritance, innate in the newborn infant's body.

After the Nazi murder of six million Jews, a more ambitious attempt to protect the Jewish community was organized, after many decades of preparation. And you might possibly think that after what had happened in World War One, and certainly after what had happened in World War Two, every thoughtful person on earth would have very seriously begun to question the value of the nation-state. Certainly the idea that a nation-state provides physical safety to its citizens would seem to have been thoroughly and decisively shown to be incorrect. All the same, many Jews had concluded even by the end of the nineteenth century that, in a world of nation-states, founding a nation-state of their own was the only way that permanent safety could ever be provided to the Jewish people, and many of the devastated Jews who were still alive after World War Two continued to pursue that objective. Most of the governments of the surviving nation-states were supportive of the idea. Governments which had coldly ignored the agony of the Jews being murdered in the camps, governments which had preferred to allow the tormented people to be gassed rather than admitting them to their own countries as refugees, now approved of giving the Jews a gift, but it was a poisoned gift—a piece of land already populated by another people. It was an act of what could be called surrogate Western imperialism, carried out just at the very moment when people all over the world were vowing to resist Western imperialism once and for all. The world allowed the state of Israel to be established in Palestine. The gift was accepted, and Israeli Jews took on a new identity. They became oppressors. So, just as the Jews had once been expelled from so many places over the preceding centuries, now Jews expelled the Palestinian Arabs from their homes and their land, and Jews, after centuries as victims of racism and injustice, learned how to practice racism and injustice themselves. Single-minded devotion to the preservation of the Jewish community had led to the subjugation of the Arab inhabitants of Palestine. And over the years and through many events, that initial subjugation has evolved into a permanent regime of arrogant cruelty, and a succession of Israeli governments have exhibited a degree of heartlessness, even of sadism, that is equal to that of many of the worst governments on earth. Of course there are many people, Jews and non-Jews, who still can't believe that this is the case and who try not to learn too much about the situation or to think too much about it. And then there are others who know all about it but attempt to interpret it all in a positive light.

And this brings me to the organizations whose newsletters I receive and their accusations of anti-Semitism. And in a way it's appalling that a person like myself, who has had nothing but good luck in his life and has suffered little, a person of no great emotional depth who's sitting comfortably at his table finishing an agreeable breakfast, should presume to judge or criticize the newsletters of these organizations, which are in many cases written by people who have either suffered greatly themselves or whose parents and grandparents suffered and in many cases lost their families because of the acts of anti-Semites. So, while I give myself permission to have whatever opinion seems to me right about the subjects covered in my daily newsletters, I enjoin myself at the same time to remember that what's written in them—particularly in the sections I find most impossible to accept—is written because the authors have been emotionally harried, wounded, and twisted by the anguish inflicted on earlier generations of their families. Marx used the wonderful phrase "congealed labor" to remind us of the workers whose difficult struggle was inextricably baked into the physical objects we casually use every day, and we can say about the newsletters sent out by these organizations that their sentences contain the congealed terror and the congealed grief of generations of persecuted people. For that reason, we need to remind ourselves not to derive too much enjoyment from uncovering the possible fallacies and sophistries of these haunted writers.

The general well-meaning public in the generation before mine, overwhelmed by shame over what had been allowed to happen to the Jews during World War Two, accepted without question many of the assumptions still shared by the writers of these newsletters. And of course there's a sort of triumphant, transgressive pleasure that can come to us when we defy what was the conventional wisdom of the previous generation, particularly a previous generation that contained a large quantity of self-satisfied people who had a complacently benign attitude towards the world but ignored a lot of things. But that pleasure is itself self-satisfied and preposterously self-congratulatory. Let's try to remember that the whole story is tragic.

If your view of the world is that there are Jews and then there are non-Jews, and if your view of your role in life is that you are a defender of the Jews, then if non-Jews are denouncing Jews, you may not pay that much attention to which Jews are being denounced and the various reasons the non-Jews give for their denunciations. And indeed the central mandate of the organizations whose newsletters I receive is to ignore those distinctions with steely determination. But from any perspective on life other than theirs, the distinctions matter. Hitler denounced Jews because he believed in an insane fantasy about race.

Contemporary Palestinians denounce the Israelis because the Israelis have stolen their land, killed their children, bulldozed their homes, made their daily lives unbearable, and starved them. To accuse contemporary Palestinians of anti-Semitism would be almost funny, as if one had said that Jews despised Hitler because they had an anti-Austrian prejudice.

In other words, some of the writers of the newsletters have drawn from the centuries-long history of murderous anti-Semitism the conclusion that anti-Semitism is a sort of eternal force that merely changes its face over time but will never go away. The Jews had not poisoned the wells in twelfth century France, nor had they caused Germany's defeat in World War One, and yet people had blamed them and wanted to kill them, and so, they believe, the story is continuing in the same fashion today. As they see it, today's Palestinians are part of an eternal army opposing the Jews, and when violent action is taken by Israel, and Palestinian children are killed, the number of those killed, from this point of view, seems trivial compared to the number gassed by Hitler in an earlier battle.

So then we have to consider the fact that there are unusual individuals in every country who habitually stand on the side of the un-privileged, the un-lucky, the weak, and the subjugated. And these defenders of the weak can often be particularly courageous people. Some of them routinely risk prison and even death because of standing up for oppressed people. And indeed, one might well say that these champions of the un-privileged are among the most admirable people in every country. And yet, consistently, because of their sympathy and support for the Palestinians, these are the very people repeatedly singled out for contempt and vilified as anti-Semites in my daily newsletters, even though no one can point to any particular things that they've said or actions that they've taken that would indicate that they have a particular prejudice against Jews or that their support for the Palestinians is based on a prejudice against Jews.

Many of them are Jews themselves, almost all of them work side by side every day with Jews, and a few of them even have pictures of Jews like Karl Marx hanging on their walls.

The accusation of anti-Semitism is a terrible and terrifying accusation. It casts a cloud of suspicion and doubt around a person that may be almost impossible to dispel, because the rumor that any given person secretly harbors a horrible and revolting inner hatred is weirdly easy to believe and impossible to decisively disprove. And the very word "anti-Semite" carries the association of the gas chambers and crematoria of Auschwitz, and it places the person accused of it in the same category as those who slaughtered six million people.

Because human beings are mysterious entities, or I would say fundamentally unknowable, it was easy, in medieval times, for a Christian to subject his neighbor, a Jew, to an entirely superstitious, utterly unscientific, and completely subjective form of observation and to conclude that the neighbor had literally made a personal arrangement with the Devil and had agreed to do the Devil's bidding on earth, and it's easy today for any one of us to suspect that our neighbor shows signs of prejudice, and in the right circumstances it's not hard to convince others to share our suspicions. Prejudice comes of course in many flavors. There's a spectrum that runs all the way from ignoring or vaguely not noticing members of a certain group all the way on up through mild disdain, distaste, disgust, fear, horror, and loathing. And for those who move through the world with the sense that a large proportion of the people they meet feel a certain disdain for them, much less some variety of disgust or loathing, life can become exhausting and demoralizing and eventually even unbearable. The problem is that, because we all grew up in a world full of prejudice, and because we are all victims of our own not-conscious minds, and because we do not have the ability to easily transform ourselves into the people we'd ideally like to be, we are all at least a little bit prejudiced towards various well-defined or ill-defined groups. Quite apart from groups coming from different ancestries, we have irrational feelings about people who are by some standard overweight or people who are short or people whose way of pronouncing certain sounds in certain words is slightly abnormal and to us infuriating. So prejudice is very real. And those of us who belong to groups that have frequently been disliked or despised can't lightly dismiss the suggestion that a given individual may be prejudiced against our group. Under certain circumstances, we can easily begin to feel more and more convinced that a certain person, or two people, or a lot of people, are looking down on us, and we can even persuade others in our group to feel the same. And history tells us that some who have had such suspicions have basically been right. But it's also possible to feel that way and be basically wrong.

Of course the more we believe that our group is the object of prejudice, and the closer our identification becomes with the group, the greater is the danger that we will incorrectly believe ourselves to have more in common with the other members of our group than we really have, and less in common with individuals outside the group than we really have. And the truth is that we humans are not only not good at making guesses about the inner life of our fellow humans, we are absolutely terrible at it. We're wrong even about those we know well, those we live with and see every day. And so, yes, if a certain individual makes anti-Jewish statements or jokes, or if they discriminate against Jews in their personal or professional behavior, then undoubtedly we can feel confident in considering them to one degree or another anti-Semitic. But when we try to speculate about individuals apart from their words and their deeds, when we try to guess what they feel inside, we may very well be wrong about them. And even if we're one percent right, and a tiny drop of prejudice against us still sloshes around in the vast basement of a certain person's mind, our own unconscious minds are not entirely free of prejudice either, and we may need to rise above our possibly-true speculation. It's terrible to make the mistake of categorizing as an enemy someone who in fact is a good-hearted person who could potentially be a friend.

A lot of what we consider human progress has occurred because various individual members of mistreated groups identified passionately with their group and figured out how to fight for their group. If human beings had lacked the capacity for group identification, if human individuals had lacked the ability to see that they and their neighbor were both suffering under the same intolerable conditions, all of us today would probably be living as slaves under one or another pharaoh, and there would be no hope for anything better for us. All the same, to form an unconditional bond with a collective entity—to answer the question "What am I?" by referring to a "race," a nation, a group, a community—is always a very dangerous choice. In other words, in my opinion the B Minor Mass of Johann Sebastian Bach is great. And in my opinion Angela Merkel's decision to welcome the Syrian refugees in 2015 was great. But I don't think that "Germany" is great. I don't think "the German people" are great. I don't think "the United States" is great. I don't think "the American people" are great. I don't think "Great Britain" is great. And I don't think "the British people" are great. No nation is great, and no group of people is great. A passionate admiration for one's own group can somewhat easily turn into some kind of contempt for others, and if one is speaking of "races" or national groups, it can even sometimes lead to the very type of racist contempt for others that was intertwined with Western imperialism and slavery, as well as countless cases of the slaughter of the innocent down to our own day.

And so as I sit here reading my daily newsletters, I find myself gesturing frantically at my breakfast table. I feel almost desperate. I want to speak out loud to the writer of each article I'm reading, to say I know, I know, each step you took in your reasoning over the course of your life was understandable, and each step made sense—in a way. But look at where you've ended up—you're drowning in injustice, you're defending hideous cruelty, and you're heaping abuse every day on some of the world's most admirable human beings, people who are not even your enemies. Somehow your thinking must have taken a wrong turn.

First of all, you distanced yourselves from all the other victims of racism and remorseless mass murder that have occurred in our world. Rather than identifying with other victims and trying to comprehend the mechanisms that might lie behind all such cases, you insisted on the uniqueness of the Jewish case. Of course there's no doubt that the Jewish case is unique in its nature, in its scale, and in its long twisted history. But can you explain what happened to the Rohingya in Burma in 2016 and 2017 or to the Tutsi in Rwanda in 1994? No, you can't, because each of those cases of racism is also unique, and in fact most cases of racism have unique, long, and twisted histories behind them.

You consistently use a phrase that insists on the separateness of the Jewish case, the phrase "racism and anti-Semitism." That phrase doesn't help us at all in any quest for insight, and it ought to be abandoned.

As self-appointed defenders of Israel, you don't understand why the countries of the world so often vote against Israel in the United Nations and why young people all over the world march in demonstrations against Israel and why so many thoughtful older people are irritated and annoyed by you, the supporters of Israel. Or you simply conclude that this is the way non-Jews have always felt about Jews, it's based on the same eternal prejudice, and there's no need for you to think seriously about it. And it's true that people born in the last seventy years or so may or may not be vividly aware of what happened to the Jewish people in earlier years. But the fact is that if asked to list the groups that have been most tormented during the time that they themselves have been alive, they are likely to mention the people of Vietnam, the people of Iraq, the people of Syria, and many other groups of people, before they mention either Jews around the world or the citizens of Israel, and this is why they don't accept the way that you seem to claim a unique moral authority, as victims, to be above criticism.

Unfortunately, it's sad but true that, in part precisely because it so assiduously defends its right to commit the crimes it commits, Israel, very much like apartheid-era South Africa in its day, has become a country that is looked upon with almost unquestioned disdain by people around the world who care about protecting the unprotected and the weak. Some of these people may know a great deal about the current situation in Israel and the Palestinian territories and all the history that led up to the current moment, and some may know very little. But they are not wrong in seeing, for example, the shooting of unarmed protesters and the ghastly collective punishment of almost two million people in Gaza as among the current world's most vicious, systematic, and merciless attempts to dominate or crush a defenseless population. And they resent the techniques you use every day—the endless and varied ways in which you wield the accusation of anti-Semitism—to stop people from criticizing either the state of Israel or you, its tireless defenders.

You've really established a preposterous set of rules for anyone who wants to talk or write about this particular subject, and you know just what to say if these rules are broken. If someone wants to criticize a Jewish politician in the United States, for example, if someone wants to say, Well, this particular politician always seems to defend Israel no matter what it does, he uses very deceitful and dishonest arguments and rhetoric, and by the way he receives a large part of his campaign funding from wealthy supporters of Israel, you will reply by saying, Well, the person who says that is clearly anti-Semitic because they're using ancient and obvious anti-Semitic slurs; they're saying that this fine politician is more "loyal" to the Jewish people and Israel than he is to his own country, they're calling him "tricky" and "sneaky," and they're saying that rich Jews use their money to try to buy influence, bend people to their will, and control things. And so you do your best to force everyone to talk about whether what's been said about the politician does or does not echo things that anti-Semites said in various past centuries, and you hope that everyone forgets about the fact that what was said about the politician may simply be true.

You say that people who discuss the negative consequences of the founding of the state of Israel are anti-Semitic, because in mentioning those consequences they're implying that Jews, and only Jews, had no right to found a state and no right of self-determination, and you say that people who criticize the actions of the state of Israel are anti-Semitic because they hold Israel to a standard of behavior higher than what is asked of any other country. Well, obviously, the hope of various groups to have a nation-state of their own, from the Kurds to the Basques and on and on, forms one of the endless painful themes of political history, but it's unusual for a group to select a location for their nation-state where they themselves mostly don't live and where other people do live. And it's hardly true that Israel is held to a higher standard than other countries. People who think about what's happening in the world savagely criticize countries other than Israel every hour of every day. They savagely criticize the United States, and in particular its founding. They savagely criticize Russia. They savagely criticize China. But the accusations of anti-Semitism still sting and can still dominate the conversation. They're arrows whose poison never seems to wear off.

Your obsession with the daily defense of every choice made by the Israeli state is perhaps a consequence of the fact that you're still reacting much too literal-mindedly to the statements that various ignorant and malevolent people made to your ancestors long ago. The ignorant and malevolent people said, You are Jews, you use the blood of children in rituals, you poison wells, and we're going to kill you, we're going to kill you because you're Jews. And then they tried to kill your ancestors, and they killed millions. But because of their terrible success, you took what they said too seriously. They said, The problem is Jews, we hate Jews, so you thought the problem was all about Jews and the hatred of Jews. No—that was a mistake. Anti-Semitism was never really about Jews.

People don't need to know a great deal about Jews in order to be anti-Semites. In fact, they don't need to know anything. Most anti-Semites have known little or nothing about Jews. Many have never encountered a Jew. You think they hate Jews, and then they try to kill them. No. The truth is that in order for people to kill Jews, they don't need to hate them. They might hate them, or they might not hate them, or they might not be sure. But whether one looks at the Middle Ages or at Nazified Europe, the Jews weren't killed because they were Jews. They weren't killed because of any trait they possessed. They weren't killed because people hated them. They were killed because history created certain circumstances in which one or another population grew desperate, and, maddened by desperation, sometimes under the sway of demonic leaders, sometimes not, they felt driven to blame a weaker group of people for their problems and their misery. Looking for an appropriate weaker group to blame, the deluded population looked around them, and in Europe the Jews were for centuries by far the most obvious target, because they were easily identifiable, they were alien and mysterious to those outside their community, and they were defenseless. And so the deluded population blamed them, and then they tormented them, and then they killed them.

This is why in a way it really isn't important whether Adolf Eichmann hated Jews or didn't hate them. Maybe he hated them on Monday, and on Tuesday he didn't care. He would have been up to his neck in killing them whether he hated them or not. If Franz Kafka had gone to meet Eichmann in his office, would Eichmann have hated him? We have no idea. In fact, we'll never know what sorts of odd, bizarre ideas were floating around in Eichmann's head. He organized transports of Jews to be killed. He wanted to kill Jews. But the Jews that Eichmann wanted to kill or that the citizens of Blois wanted to kill in 1171 were not the suffering human beings they actually killed. The Jews they wanted to kill were made-up fantasy characters. If the best-known and most accessible minority group in twentieth-century Europe had been the Armenians or the Kurds, Adolf Hitler might well have become fixated on the Armenians or the Kurds, and he might well have tried to kill the Armenians or the Kurds. And this is why, yes, it was kind of, sort of, great that after World War Two many Germans who would formerly have vilified "the Jews" came to realize that the Jews were not bad people, and concert-goers in Munich cheered Leonard Bernstein. And similarly, in a way, it was kind of, sort of, great that as recent decades passed, many Americans who'd once been very prejudiced against anyone seen as "black" became more accepting of people of color and even elected one to be President of the country. These were victories, and they may have saved lives. But from another point of view they were small victories, because the problem with the human species is not that some people in Germany don't like Jews, and some people in the United States don't like people with dark skin, and some people in Egypt don't like Coptic Christians, and some people in Africa don't like men who love other men, and some people in Mexico don't like transgender women, and some people in Indonesia don't like Communists, and some people in Hungary don't like immigrants. The problem is that human beings make up categories, put each other into them, and then, they turn the people in some of those categories into made-up fantasy characters, and then, when times are bad, when circumstances are bad, they persecute those people and kill them. And this is why the problem isn't solved simply by trying to defend Jews.

The horrors caused by the warming of the climate can to some extent be predicted, as can the horrors caused by an uncontrolled disease. The processes that create these problems are to a certain extent understood by science. The opposite is true for the horrors that flow from racism. We can't predict them, and we're quite far from understanding them, even though, paradoxically, the developments in the climate and the dangerous diseases come at us from the outside, and racism is a force with which we're intimately familiar, because some of its currents flow right through us. How close are we to understanding the economic, sociological, and political conditions that create racism in the first place? And how close are we to fully understanding what the historical circumstances are that can turn racism—or prejudice, suspicion, and fear—into a drive towards violence? We don't understand the murder of old people and children by American soldiers in Vietnam. We don't understand why Robert Bowers, a citizen of Pennsylvania who'd drawn little attention from his neighbors for forty-six years, suddenly drove to a synagogue outside Pittsburgh one morning in 2018 and killed eleven worshippers there. We don't know what was going on in the mind of the Minneapolis policeman, Derek Chauvin, who kneeled on the neck of George Floyd for minute after minute until he was dead. And in the very same way, we simply do not understand the murder of the six million Jews in the 1940's. We don't understand it. We can read and reread the facts of the case, just as we can endlessly stare at photographs of the impassive faces of Robert Bowers and Derek Chauvin, but there's a mystery, a locked box, at the center of these stories. Perhaps by comparing them all, by studying them all at once, we might be able to make some progress in understanding them. But until we do, we live in terrible fear of ourselves, never knowing when one of us, or some of us, may strike. Because unfortunately something is wrong with us. We are not healthily functioning animals. Injustice and misery drive us all too easily into madness, and injustice and misery are everywhere.

Reading Plays
1997

On the one hand, there's something rather strange about the idea of reading plays. You could certainly say that what a play is, really, is what actors do together in front of an audience—or a one-person play is what one actor does alone in front of an audience. When you see a play, you see people, members of your own species, engaged in their ordinary physical life in front of you—walking, sitting, digesting, growing older, talking to each other, perhaps touching each other. Their names, in the play, are not their "real" names, maybe, and the words they say to each other may previously have been "written"—but a play is basically a physical experience, for the actors and for you, and most of what you're seeing is exactly what you seem to be seeing—the actors *are* talking, they *are* touching, they're thinking, they're feeling things, they're living in front of you a certain portion of their lives that will never come again. The previously written dialogue drives the actors to experiment with saying what is *not* true. The dialogue forces the actor to practice the human skill of lying. And actors do perfect that skill and can become extraordinarily convincing. Sometimes the actors conspire together to fool the audience with lies that everyone knows are lies. One actor says to another, "I just swallowed poison," and that is a lie, and both of them know it, although you in the audience are in some sense fooled. But part of the fascination of theatre comes from the fact that the actors are not always lying. Sometimes one actor may say to another, "I hate you! I hate you!" and the other actor wonders if it might be true, or believes it *is*, while the actor who says it may be secretly thinking, as we do in life, "Could this possibly be what I really mean?" Our daily pretense that we know who we are is abandoned by the actors, who are led by the dialogue to try out the possibility that what they think and feel is not limited by prior decisions about "who they are" or the supposed outlines of their supposed biographies. The dialogue leads the actor who, in daily life, is known as "sensitive" to become, for a while, insensitive instead, while the actor whose acquaintances call him cold becomes warm and compassionate. The dialogue of a play is part of an elaborate network of personal events in the lives of the actors, just as our own dialogue is in our own daily lives.

It is strange, then, to isolate the dialogue of a play in a book, and it's strange to read it—to sit somewhere alone and read it silently to yourself. Reading a recipe is not the same as eating a cake. Reading about lovemaking is not the same as making love.

And yet, on the other hand, one has to say that a written play can have a special magic of its own. Reading a recipe may only remind you of the cake that you wish you could have in front of you, but reading a play can be a rather complete experience. The written play has its own music, its own very pristine existence—words, thoughts, and spirit abstracted from the physical, abstracted from the bodies of actors and their travails through space. There are wonderful things that can happen in the mind of a reader that cannot happen to anyone watching actors in a play. Indeed, the actors are often aspiring, as they act, to approach, in physical reality, the experience they had originally when they themselves read the play—but, as the reading experience is in an entirely different realm, they can never quite manage to hit that target (just as writers may often, with an equal degree of un-success—for the very same reason—attempt to capture in words a powerful mood or a feeling that overwhelmed them in life).

More and more I've come to think (perhaps you'll find this self-serving) that to call plays or stories or poems "good" or "bad" is often not very illuminating, whereas it can at times be extremely helpful to notice that "right now, when I read these particular poems, I feel well, I feel happy, I feel that I am getting something that I have needed." It's not that those poems are "the best" poems or that they're "better" than certain others, but that for you, now, they are important and right. Animals in the forest require certain nutrients, and they learn how to find them. They don't all need the same things, and they don't need the same things at every stage in their lives. The nuts that a particular badger finds of very little value may turn out to be crucial for a particular squirrel. As writers, we can't predict who might come along who might find our offerings valuable. But because we've all been readers, we know what the experience is like, and we hope that what certain writers have given to us, we will give to someone.

Interview with Noam Chomsky 2004

September 17, 2004, Noam Chomsky's office in the Department of Linguistics and Philosophy at M.I.T.

Wallace Shawn: A lot of what you've written has to do with the ways in which human beings use their minds—use their very capacity for rationality, one could say—not to seek truth, but on the contrary to distort truth, to twist truth, often so as to justify various crimes they want to commit or have already committed. And this doesn't have to do so much with our personal behavior but with our behavior in groups. So-called leaders dream up the justifications, and everybody else absorbs and accepts them.

Noam Chomsky: It's simply very easy to subordinate oneself to a worldview that's supportive of one's own interests. Most of us don't go around murdering people or stealing food from children. There are a lot of activities that we just regard as pathological when we do them individually. On the other hand, when they're done collectively, they're considered necessary and appropriate. Clinton, Kennedy: they all carried out mass murder, but they didn't think that that was what they were doing—nor does Bush. You know, they were defending justice and democracy from greater evils. And in fact I think you'd find it hard to discover a mass murderer in history who didn't think that . . . It's kind of interesting to read the Russian archives, which are coming out now. They're being sold, like everything in Russia, and so we're learning something about the internal discussions of the Russian leaders, and they talked to each other the same way they talked publicly. I mean, these gangsters, you know, who were taking over Eastern Europe in the late '40s and early '50s—they were talking to each other soberly about how we have to defend East European democracy from the fascists who are trying to undermine it. It's pretty much the public rhetoric, and I don't doubt that they believed it.

WS: But one has to say about human beings—well, human beings did manage to invent the concepts of truth and falsity, and that's a remarkable accomplishment. And surely if people really used the concepts of truth and falsity rigorously, if they applied the laws of rationality rigorously, they would be forced to confront the true nature of the things they might be planning to do, and that might be enough to prevent them from doing many terrible things. After all, most justifications for mass murder flatly contradict the perpetrator's professed beliefs—and are based on factually false assumptions as well. Couldn't education somehow lead people to use their capacity for rational thought on a more regular basis, to take rationality more seriously? So that they *couldn't* accept absurd justifications for things? As we're sitting here in the Department of Linguistics and Philosophy, wouldn't it benefit the world if more people studied philosophy?

NC: Take Heidegger, one of the leading philosophers of the twentieth century. I mean, just read his straight philosophical work, *An Introduction to Metaphysics*. A few pages in, it starts off with the Greeks, as the origins of civilization, and the Germans as the inheritors of the Greeks, and we have to protect the Greek heritage . . . This was written in 1935. The most civilized people in the West, namely the Germans—Germany was the most educated country in the world—the Germans were coming under the delusion that their existence, and in fact the existence of Western civilization since the Greeks, was threatened by fierce enemies against whom they had to protect themselves.

I mean, it was deeply imbued in the general culture—in part

including German Jews. There's a book by a major humanistic figure of modern Jewish life, Joachim Prinz. He was in Germany in the '30s, and he wrote a book called *Wir Juden* (We Jews), in which he said, Look, we don't like the anti-Semitic undertones of what the Nazis are doing, but we should bear in mind that much of what they're saying is right, and we agree with it. In particular their emphasis on blood and land—*Blut und Boden*. Basically we agree with that. We think that the identity of blood is very important, and the emphasis on the land is very important. And the tie between blood and land is important. And in fact as late as 1941, influential figures in the Jewish Palestinian community, the pre-state community, including the group that included Yitzhak Shamir, who later became prime minister, sent a delegation to try to reach the German government, to tell them that they would like to make an arrangement with the Germans, and they would be the outpost for Germany in the Middle East, because they basically agreed with them on a lot of things. Now, no one would suggest this was the mainstream, by any means, but it also wasn't a pathological fringe. Or take Roosevelt. Roosevelt was always quite pro-Fascist, thought Mussolini was "that admirable Italian gentleman," as he called him. As late as 1939, he was saying that Fascism was an important experiment that they were carrying out, until it was distorted by the relation to Hitler. And this was almost twenty years after they destroyed the Parliament, broke up the labor movement, raided Ethiopia with all the atrocities . . .

WS: A lot of people feel that hope for humanity lies not so much in the progress of rationality but rather in the possibility that more people will fall under the influence of moral principles or moral codes, such as the ethical systems developed by various religions. After all, if everyone were seriously committed to moral ideals, then . . .

NC: Moral codes . . . you can find things in the traditional religions that are very benign and decent and wonderful and so on, but I mean, the Bible is probably the most genocidal book in the literary canon. The God of the Bible—not only did he order His chosen people to carry out literal genocide—I mean, wipe out every Amalekite to the last man, woman, child, and, you know, donkey and so on, because hundreds of years ago they got in your way when you were trying to cross the desert—not only did He do things like that, but, after all, the God of the Bible was ready to destroy every living creature on earth because some humans irritated Him. That's the story of Noah. I mean, that's *beyond* genocide—you don't know how to describe this creature. Somebody offended Him, and He was going to destroy every living being on earth? And then He was talked into allowing two of each species to stay alive—that's supposed to be gentle and wonderful.

WS: Hmm . . . if moral codes themselves can't be relied upon, it's hard to know what to cling to if we want to avoid falling into moral nightmares . . . In a way, it seems to be simply our obsessive need to have a high opinion of ourselves that leads us repeatedly into idiotic thinking. If our vestigial rationality detects a conflict between our actions and our principles—well, we don't want to change our actions, and it's embarrassing to change our principles, so we wield the blowtorch against our rationality, bending it till it's willing to say that our principles and actions are well-aligned. We're prisoners of self-love.

NC: We understand the crimes of others but can't understand our own. Take that picture over there on the wall. What it is, is the Angel of Death, obviously. Off on the right is Archbishop Romero, who was assassinated in 1980. The figures below are the six leading Jesuit intellectuals who had their brains blown out in 1989, and their housekeeper and her daughter, who were also murdered. Now, they were murdered by an elite battalion armed, trained, and directed by the United States. The archbishop was murdered pretty much by the same hands. Well, a couple of weeks ago there was a court case in California where some members of the family of Romero brought some kind of a civil suit against one of the likely killers and actually won their case. Well, that's a pretty important precedent, but it was barely reported in the United States. Nobody wants to listen. You know, Czeslaw Milosz was a courageous, good person. And when he died there were huge stories. But he and his associates faced nothing in Eastern Europe like what intellectuals faced in our domains. I mean, Havel was put in jail. He didn't have his brains blown out by elite battalions trained by the Russians. In Rwanda, for about a hundred days they were killing about eight thousand people a day. And we just went through the tenth anniversary. There was a lot of lamentation about how we didn't do anything about it, and how awful, and we ought to do something about other people's crimes, and so on. That's an easy one—to do something about other people's crimes. But you know, every single day, about the same number of people—children—are dying in Southern Africa from easily treatable diseases. Are we doing anything about it? I mean, that's Rwanda-level killing, just children, just Southern Africa, every day—not a hundred days but all the time. It doesn't take military intervention. We don't need to worry about who's going to protect our forces. What it takes is bribing totalitarian institutions to produce drugs. It costs pennies. Do we think about it? Do we do it? Do we ask what kind of a civilization is it where we have to bribe totalitarian institutions in order to get them to produce drugs to stop Rwanda-level killing every day? It's just easier not to think about it.

WS: Totalitarian institutions—you mean the drug companies?

NC: Yes. What are they? The drug companies are just totalitarian institutions which are subsidized: most of the basic research is funded by the public, there are huge profits, and of course from a business point of view it not only makes sense, but it's legally required for them to produce lifestyle drugs for rich

Westerners to get rid of wrinkles, instead of malaria treatments for dying children in Africa. It's required. It's legally required.

WS: How do we get out from under that?

NC: Well, the first thing we have to do is face it. Until you face it, you can't get out from under it. Take fairly recent things like the feminist movement—women's rights. I mean, if you had asked my grandmother if she was oppressed she would have said no. She wouldn't have known what you were talking about. Of course she was stuck in the kitchen all day, and she followed orders. And the idea that her husband would do anything around the house . . . I mean, my mother would not *allow* my father, or me, for that matter, into the kitchen. Literally. Because we were supposed to be studying the Talmud or something. But did they think they were oppressed? Well, actually, my mother already felt that she was. But my grandmother didn't. And to get that awareness—you know, it's not easy.

India is interesting in this respect. There have been some very careful studies, and one of the best was about the province of Uttar Pradesh. It has one of the lowest female to male ratios in the world, not because of female infanticide, but because of the shitty way women are treated. And I mean, I was shocked to discover that in the town where I live, Lexington, which is a professional, upper-middle-class community—you know, doctors, lawyers, academics, stockbrokers, mostly that sort of thing—the police have a special unit for domestic abuse which has two or three 911 calls a week. Now, you know, that's important. Because thirty years ago, they *didn't* have that, because domestic abuse was not considered a problem. Now at least it's considered a problem, and police forces deal with it, and the courts deal with it in some fashion. Well, you know, that takes work—it takes work to recognize that oppression is going on.

This was very striking to me in the student movement in the '60s. I mean, I was pretty close to it, and those kids were involved in something very serious. You know, they were very upset, and they hated the war, and they hated racism, and their choices weren't always the right ones by any means, but they were very emotional about it, for very good reasons . . .

I was involved particularly with the resisters, who were refusing to serve in the army. They're now called "draft evaders" and so on, but that's bullshit. I mean, almost all of them could have gotten out of the draft easily. A lot of them were theology students, and others—you'd go to your doctor, and he'd say you were a homosexual or something. It was nothing for a privileged kid to get out of the army if he wanted to. They were *choosing* to resist. And facing serious penalties. For an eighteen-year-old kid to go to jail for years or live their life in exile was not an easy choice—especially when, of course, if you conformed, you would just shoot up there and be part of the elite. But they chose it, and it was a courageous decision, and they were denounced for it and condemned for it and so on . . . At some stage of the game, the feminist movement began. In the early stages of the resistance, the women were supposed to be supportive, you know, to these resisters. And at some stage these young women began to ask, Why are we doing the shit work? I mean, why are we the ones who are supposed to look up in awe at *them*, when we're doing most of the work? And they began to regard themselves as being oppressed. Now that caused a rather serious psychological problem for the boys. Because they thought, and rightly, that they were doing something courageous and noble, and here suddenly they had to face up to the fact that they were oppressors, and that was hard. I mean, I know people who committed suicide. Literally. Because they couldn't face it.

So, just in our lifetime, it's different. The kinds of things that were considered normal—not just normal, unnoticeable, you didn't see them—thirty or forty years ago, would be unspeakable now. The same with gay rights. There have been big changes in consciousness, and they're important, and they make it a better world. But they do not affect *class* issues. Class is a dirty word in the United States. You can't talk about it.

One of my daughters teaches in a state college in which the aspirations of most of the students are to become a nurse or a policeman. The first day of class (she teaches history) she usually asks her students to identify their class background. And it turns out there are two answers. Either they're middle class, or they're [part of the] underclass. If their father has a job, like as a janitor, they're middle class. If their father is in jail or transient, then it's underclass. That's it. Nobody's working class. It's just not a concept that exists. It's not just here—it's true in England too. I was in England a couple of months ago at the time of the Cannes Festival, when Michael Moore won, and one of the papers had a long interview with him, and the interviewer was suggesting that Michael Moore wasn't telling the truth when he said he came from a working-class background. He said he came from a working-class background, but his father had a car and owned a house, so, you know, what's this crap about coming from a working-class background? Well, his father was an auto worker! I mean, the whole concept of class in any meaningful sense has just been driven out of people's heads. The fact that there are some people who give the orders and others who follow them—that is gone. And the only question is, How many goods do you have?—as if, if you have goods, you have to be middle class, even if you're just following orders.

WS: What you possess determines how people see you and how you see yourself. That defines you—your role in the social structure does not.

NC: People are trained—and massive efforts go into this—people are trained to perceive their identity and their aspirations and their value as people in terms of the things they amass. Nothing else. And in terms of *yourself*, not anyone else . . . It's kind of interesting to watch this campaign against Social Security going on, and to see the attitudes. I see it even among students. And the reason certain people hate Social Security so much is not just that if you privatize it, it's a bonanza for Wall Street. I'm sure that's part of it, but the main reason for the real visceral hatred of Social Security is that it's based on a principle that they want to drive out of people's heads—namely, that you care about somebody else. You know, Social Security is based on the idea that you care whether the disabled widow on the other side of town has enough food to eat. And you're not supposed to think that. That's a dangerous sentiment. You're supposed to just be out for yourself. And I get this from young people now. They say, Look, I don't see why I should be responsible for her. I'm not responsible for her. I didn't do anything to her. I mean, if she didn't invest properly or, you know, something like that, that's not my business. Why do I have to pay my taxes to keep her alive? And why do I care if the kid down the street can't go to school? I mean, *I* didn't keep him from going to school.

WS: But isn't that sort of demonstrably absurd? I mean, the student who doesn't think he's involved with those other people is simply wrong. He's not a self-created atom. He's a part of society and was created by society. He didn't become whatever he is simply through his own individual efforts. It was society that gave him everything he has and everything he's ever used to become what he is. In order to become what he is, he used the English language, he used the U.S. medical system, electricity, the telephone. He didn't invent the English language. He didn't invent the telephone.

NC: Yes, but people are very deluded about this, including professionals. Take professional economists. Most of them literally believe what Alan Greenspan and others talk about—that the economy flourishes because of entrepreneurial initiative and consumer choice and so on and so forth. You know, that's total bullshit. The economy flourishes because we have a dynamic state sector.

WS: You mean, the motor driving it all is the taxpayer's money being spent—or given away to private companies—by the state. The motor is *not* the individual consumer spending his money in the free market.

NC: Just about everything in the new economy comes out of state initiatives. I mean, what's M.I.T.? M.I.T. is overwhelmingly a taxpayer-funded institution, in which research and development is carried out at public cost and risk, and if anything comes out of it, some private corporation, like the guys who endowed this building, will get the profit from it. And almost everything works like that—from computers, the Internet, telecommunications, pharmaceuticals—you run through the dynamic parts of the economy, that's where they come from. I mean, with things like, say, computers and the Internet, for example, consumer choice had no role at all! Consumers didn't even know these things existed until they'd been developed for years at public expense. But we live in a world of illusion.

WS: People's view of how it's all working is wrong. And of course most people are just totally immersed intellectually in their own personal economic struggle—their struggle to get, basically, things. But you know, when you say that people are trained to focus their aspirations entirely on things—goods—well, that has terrifying implications. To say that people may not even be aware that their lives consist of following orders—that's terrifying. It's as if people don't acknowledge that their ability to make choices about their lives, their degree of power over their own environment, is an important issue.

NC: No, what you're taught from infancy is that the only choices you're supposed to make are choices of commodities. It's none of your business how the government works or what government policies are or how the community's organized or anything else. Your job is to purchase commodities. A lot of it's conscious. There's a conscious strain in sort of liberal, intellectual thought, it goes way back, that the people really don't have any right to participate in the political system. They are supposed to choose among the responsible men.

WS: But it's funny that the people themselves go along with it, because it seems insulting. Why aren't people more insulted? They're not even insulted when they're blatantly lied to! They seem to laugh it off. But in their own lives, in daily life, people would resent it a lot—you know, being lied to.

NC: No—not when people in power lie to you. Somehow there's some law that that's the way it works.

WS: Yes . . . I feel like saying that your approach to discussing these things is a bit like the approach of a sculptor—with hammer and chisel you attack the big block of marble, and from a certain point of view, all your gestures could be seen as rather hostile or aggressive as you pursue the somewhat negative activity of cutting down the stone, but in the end something rather glorious is revealed. I think you're suggesting that to live in illusion, to be a slave to the worldview of your time and place, or to be all your life a follower of orders—these are all in a way different forms of oppression. But I think you're suggesting that all human beings have the capacity to collaborate in the task of guiding their own lives—and the life of the place where they work, the life of their community, the life of the world. It would be so amazing if people could take that possibility seriously.

Myself and How I Got into the Theatre
1996

I would love to say something useful about my plays. Unfortunately, the only thing that really seems to connect them is the fact that I wrote them, but the plays I've written don't particularly seem to reflect the person I know myself to be (or think myself to be)—except perhaps insofar as I may have decided to rearrange myself to conform to them after the fact. But if I'm going to say something about how my plays came to have the particular qualities they have, where else can I begin but with some biographical hints?

I grew up in New York City, and as I suppose anyone can tell in two seconds if they meet me, I am what people call a "child of privilege." This is the defining fact about me, and it always will be, and if I live to be two hundred years old, I'll never be able to erase the traces of it. Like everyone else who comes from that particular tribe, the children of the privileged, I was brought up to believe in the central belief of the tribe: that there's a certain (large) quantity of the world's fruits that is the appropriate portion of the children of the privileged. But I came from a family that was a "liberal" family, so, rather confusingly, I was encouraged to feel that for every dollar I took from the world, I really ought (for some reason) to "give back" a penny, at least a penny's worth of something. The unspoken and (in the case of my parents, certainly) unthought belief of the liberal privileged group was that one was supposed to be ready to rob and murder in order to secure one's appropriate portion, but as one rode off from the conquest one was always to remember to toss back to the victims a small offering, a small scrap torn off from what one had just taken.

Our family was privileged, but it was carefully explained to me that we were not rich, only "middle class," and so, oddly, I would need to "work for my living" rather than just receiving it automatically—in other words, the little package that was the life I'd inevitably possess would be waiting for me in the baggage room with my name written on it, but, annoyingly, it wouldn't be delivered to the house, I'd have to get into a taxi and go get it.

Despite this, I grew up lazy, and I've stayed lazy. I've always liked to eat ice cream and cake, and the line of least resistance for me has always been close to the border of sleep. When I was nine or ten, I kept an enormous mound of comic books on the floor of my bedroom, and my favorite thing was to burrow into my mound, find myself a comfortable position there, and in this wonderful swamp, which was also readable, I would reach a state that fell exactly midway between reading and napping.

As far as my connection to other people went, I was usually affectionate. I was usually fond of the people I met: the privileged. And I'm still fond of them. I know them well. It's easy for me to see them not as others might see them, as a group of people who fundamentally are all the same, because as holders of privilege they all play fundamentally the same social role, but as they see themselves: as remarkably distinct individuals with different opinions, thoughts, and characteristics. I know very well that they suffer, I know that they're lonely, they're lost, they're desperate, whatever.

On the other hand, there's always been some small element in me that is a bit less lazy and a bit less affectionate. You could say, boringly, that I've therefore often been a "person in conflict."

I've always loved making things, shaping things. I've always loved colored pencils and puppets and imaginary landscapes. The experience of inventing people and places, thinking about which phrase best expresses a thought, is more than enough to fill a lifetime for me. But occasionally my absorption in these voluptuous pleasures is interrupted by what feels like a vague but painful memory—a weird memory of people to whom I seem to have no current connection, the people for whom life is mainly about suffering and trying to survive. Perhaps it was my father, who taught me to love art, who also in some way nourished these perverse "memories." I remember once, when I was ten or so, I was riding in a taxi with him, and I drew his attention to an overweight, bizarre, rather miserable-looking boy whom we were passing in the street. I found the boy funny and was merrily laughing away at him when I turned around and was shocked to discover that my poor father had burst into tears. The sight of the boy hadn't struck him as funny, apparently, and my response to the boy had also, apparently, not made him happy.

Well, I guess you can see that a young man can't go too long without writing about his father. In any case, I will tell you about mine that he happened to be, of all things, an editor, a kind and beloved mentor to writers, and at the same time a highly respected judge of literature; and whenever my father was discussed, and it was really very often, it was always said that he had "high standards." (I mean, other people said it; God knows he never would have, because it would have seemed to him horribly pompous, and because he would have found the metaphor ridiculous and incoherent—one pictures with difficulty someone measuring something somehow with some odd device while standing on a ladder.) Unfortunately, in contrast to my father, I never really comprehended the whole concept of measuring in the first place. If *I* listened to a piece of music, saw a film, or read a book—well, I seemed to go through it all from moment to moment, somehow. I was enlightened or confused, indifferent or thrilled, and certain things were offered to me that I needed, or didn't, and then it was over, and I couldn't really remember the piece of work as a whole, much less pass judgment on it. In a way I didn't *see* the piece of work at all—I just lived inside it for a while or something. So when people said that the music or the book or the film was "good" or "bad," I usually felt that I just didn't know what they were talking about.

At the liberal schools to which my parents had sent me, judgment was not part of the daily routine. The schools proudly boasted that they gave no grades or marks, and so we ourselves were never judged or condemned; there was no "good" or "bad," the point was just to do what interested you, and that was something I could understand well. All the same, my father, at home, gentle as he was, would sometimes say of some piece of writing that had crossed his desk that it "hadn't worked out"; and yes, he even described certain people's attempts as "mistakes." And how was I supposed to deal with that? Well, I must say I didn't like the sound of those comments at all. No, it made me feel quite uncomfortable to hear comments like that, particularly as I began to feel that I might someday become a writer myself. After all, it was clear enough even to me that, just as a dancer might fall down during a performance, or a pianist might hit a bunch of wrong notes in a difficult passage, well, there were certain things in the field of poetry, say, certain things that an ignorant apprentice might very well write, which an accomplished master would *not* write, and there were people who actually could tell the difference, and my father was one of them. I couldn't simply dismiss the sorts of judgments my father passed. On the other hand, I honestly couldn't face being subjected to them.

Which brings me to the question of how I got into writing for the theatre. Well, it was not just that theatre happened to be the only branch of literature that my father personally stayed entirely away from; it was more that I could easily sense in some half-conscious way—and in New York in the late '60s, when I first started writing, it was particularly easy to sense this—I could sense that the whole field of theatre was really a strange sort of non-field, in which the whole business of "standards" just didn't apply. Theatre was a kind of void, a blank, an undefined emptiness. Because, I mean, what *is* theatre, really?

Is theatre an "art form"? Is drama an "art"? Poetry is an art. Painting is an art. But can a play seriously be compared to a poem or a painting? Can you seriously claim that a play can be compared to a string quartet? Well, certain playwrights have actually believed that theatre is an artistic field: Maeterlinck, for example, whose works I always loved, created aesthetically satisfying self-contained worlds, entirely distinct from the world we live in. Robert Wilson created textless but formally beautiful compositions on stage, giving time a shape as a composer might.

But doesn't the essence of theatre really lie not in its aesthetic possibilities but instead in its special ability to reflect the real world? Is theatre not a way of putting a frame around a picture of society, so that we may observe the operation of social forces and of the individual psychology that lies beneath them? Should theatre not be principally an attempt to search for truth?

Alternatively, one might emphasize the capacity of theatre to provide a forum, a gathering place, where society can meet and discuss its own future, its problems, and its needs. Or some might emphasize the fact that theatre is unique in its ability not merely to present ideas but to show at the same time the environment and the human situations from which those ideas spring.

But finally, though, there are many who would say that theatre really, in its essence, is a form of diversion, like striptease, clowning, or a carnival freak show, whose central goal must be to entertain.

Should a playwright be compared to a pastry chef in an expensive restaurant—one of those whose role it is to lighten the burden of an elite class by serving it agreeable and evanescent miniature delights? Or to a prostitute who soothes and comforts a client according to the client's specific desires? Is a playwright like an orator in the marketplace rousing people to action, or a preacher offering a sermon in church, or a friend who speaks at a dinner table?

And then there's the question: Can a play in a theatre intervene in the life of a person in the audience?

As I began to write my first plays, I could easily sense that, at least in my country, there were no generally shared beliefs about the purpose of theatre. The audiences, the critics, the playwrights, the actors, had reached no conclusions. One could clearly see that they gathered, they assembled, and plays were put on, but no one had decided what the plays were for.

By way of comparison, one could look at the field of music and observe a somewhat different situation. The goal and intention of certain musical performances could, for example, actually be discerned, relatively speaking, and critical judgments therefore were, relatively speaking, possible to make. People could give their views, for example, on all sorts of singers in all sorts of categories—on classical singers and folk singers, rock singers and jazz singers—and a degree of consensus could even be reached, because critics and audiences shared with the artists an understanding of what some of the criteria were in each category. Within the different categories, different rules were applied, because each one was aiming at something different, and this was a situation that caused no confusion. Everyone knew that Elly Ameling couldn't do what Billie Holiday did, but the point was, she could do something else. And everyone knew where the boundaries were. It was understood that a rock singer might scream, because it was appropriate to rock, while a folk singer might strive for a purity of tone that would be inappropriate to opera or to jazz. Particular music lovers might perhaps have been interested only in opera, but they wouldn't have ridiculed Billie Holiday.

People did not go to concert halls to hear something called "singing." The fact that human beings have the need to hear different sorts of singing, that the appetite for opera cannot be satisfied at a concert of folk music, was recognized in the musical world by the invention of categories. Different sorts of singing even took place in different buildings, with different critics in attendance. But in theatre, obviously, and most particularly in my country, there were no generally accepted categories of plays, there were only "plays." People still had different sorts of appetites for plays, but they didn't know how to find what they wanted. There was a high frustration level and no way to remedy it, as if restaurants had been forbidden by law from announcing the type of food they served, and people who loved *mattar paneer* had no choice but to try every restaurant in town until they hit on one with an Indian chef. And so there was a kind of critical chaos or critical vacuum. Individual audience members and individual critics each expressed and asserted their individual drives and feelings, their incoherent longings, as they made their way from play to play, and what resulted was like a bizarre sort of *imitation* of criticism, in which any criteria at all could be applied to any play at all—an evening of Expressionist theatre could be angrily denounced because it lacked the qualities of a Broadway musical, or Thornton Wilder could be excoriated because he didn't write like Eugene O'Neill—and so no sort of consensus could ever be reached on anything, each "opinion" was canceled out by another, and no opinion could be taken seriously.

And that all felt rather agreeable to me, because it meant that no one in theatre would be held to account; if a person wrote a play, as opposed to a poem, for example, there was not going to be any way to prove, or even plausibly to argue, that what he wrote was not good, that what he wrote was in fact a "mistake." It was a field in which one might be left alone, and I leapt into it.

(Of course, if you're actually interested to know all this, you can imagine that it was all, naturally, an unconscious process, and as is probably always the case with choices like this, my decision to get involved with "theatre" was heavily overdetermined, and among the factors were all the usual ones—childhood experiences, later experiences, schools, teachers, inclinations, for all

I know genetic predispositions. From the inside it all felt simply like a matter of instinct: I'd always loved seeing plays and, as a boy, putting on shows of different kinds; when I was twenty-four, I wrote my first full-length, grown-up play, I didn't know why; I found it very exciting, and I never stopped.)

And of course it all turned out to be awfully silly in a way, as one might have predicted. The plays I wrote were, after a few years, actually performed, and I felt very fortunate; but, to my surprise, whenever I ventured out to see one of my own plays, I was always seized by the very strong suspicion that three quarters of the audience were actually sitting there under some awful misapprehension, wondering when the bears on bicycles were going to appear. And they never appeared, and so it was all rather painful and depressing for everybody. In the rather bluntly named little universe of "non-profit" theatre in which I dwelled, people would sign up at different theatres a year in advance to see a "season" of plays, and then they would sign up year after year, and so it seemed to be always the same sad individuals wandering into my plays, again and again, hoping, hoping, hoping for something, then gradually falling into a familiar disappointment, their sadness growing heavier moment by moment, before it all somehow ended and they miserably walked away . . . I wasn't a sadist, so I didn't enjoy this. And what kind of people, I'd wonder, would insist on going through something like that, night after night? Decades passed, and there they still were. The theatre-goers.

I had decided I wanted to write for the theatre, and that meant that the people who would ultimately hear what I had to say were the theatre-goers. But who were the theatre-goers? In my country they were a very small group, because theatre in the United States has simply never caught on in the way it has in England or on the European continent, for example. Those enormous respectable crowds had never gathered in the United States, the way they had in so many European cities, to watch the plays of Ibsen or Racine. The habit simply had never been formed. For most people in the United States, the issue of theatre just didn't arise. And as for those who, somehow, *had* gone so far as to see a play or two—well, the experience had left most of them rather nonplussed. Having been exposed extensively to the rival storytelling mediums of television and film, most of my fellow-countrymen found it frankly rather peculiar to pay *extra* money to attend an event in which the faces of the actors could barely be seen, and where you had to strain to hear what on earth they were saying (despite the fact that they never stopped shouting, even when standing right next to each other). Theatre obviously was *embarrassing.* It was embarrassing from the first moment, because the actors were trying so hard to fool you, but you never were fooled. You never believed what they seemed to be begging you to believe. Despite the heavy frock coats and the funny hats under which you imagined them sweating, despite the recorded sounds of horses' hooves, sleighbells, and the cracking of the whip, when the actors walked off the stage, you never believed they were going to Kharkhov.

So the theatre-goers in the United States—the loyal followers of theatre, the ones who, despite everything, loved the theatre—the theatre-goers were an odd little circle, a funny old group. Not the sophisticates, one would have to say. Not people who listened to Hugo Wolf or George Crumb or Charlie Parker on their evenings off from the theatre. Not the aesthetes, with their well-worn copies of Kawabata and George Herbert. And, of course, not anyone who was poor or desperate or hungry or oppressed, because theatre is only for the middle class. (People frequently insist, and I suppose I believe it, that in their own times the plays of Shakespeare and Sophocles were part of the life of rich and poor alike, but times have changed, and we have to say that theatre today is very definitely not for everyone. Music is for everyone. Everyone, from the richest of the rich to the poorest of the poor, listens to music. But theatre is only for the middle class.) And in a way these sad wanderers, the lovers of theatre, doggedly attached to a form from the past, for all sorts of reasons unable to take pleasure in the loud, glittering forms of the present, were "my people," to use that phrase that nationalists and tribalists sometimes employ—they were "my people" in that I too loved to sit in a theatre and watch actors act, to follow the story, to listen to the dialogue; I too loved the darkened auditorium, the moment of ecstasy before the play begins; I adored it all, every bit of it. I shared with the group an addiction, a taste, a fetish, a need. It was only in the matter of our preferred "content" that we sometimes parted company. Because I was only mildly drawn to the prewar archetype of bourgeois theatre—elegant aristocrats winking at each other in evening dress—and even less fascinated by the postwar type—animalistic louts roaring and bellowing like wounded beasts. Those worlds on stage didn't really interest me that much. I mean, the aristocrats or the louts would have interested me a lot in real life, or, if I'd seen a documentary about them, I would have been utterly engrossed. It was the fantasies that didn't mean very much to me. They were not my fantasies.

I was in a world—theatre—that was not quite my world. And so as I embarked on a life of writing for the theatre, I felt I was writing, in a way, for no one, because I couldn't help feeling that what I cared about, what I thought about, what I read about, and even the artistic works that were important to me, would all quite possibly be of very little interest to most of the people who would be coming to see my plays.

Now, if you write with the expectation that what you say will be heard and understood, then you and your audience are actually involved in a common endeavor, and while you're writing, they're sitting there beside you, helping you to know how best to reach them. And this help is a wonderful thing. If you're writing to "make your living" as well, a further valuable discipline asserts itself, because the more successful you are in speaking to your audience directly and clearly, the nicer the life you'll be able to lead. This is called the discipline of the market, and it can indeed drive people to accomplish things they couldn't have accomplished without it.

Well, I didn't expect to be understood, and I quickly realized that I'd never be able to "make my living" as a writer of plays (assuming as I did, without ever thinking about it, that my "living" obviously had to include at least the minimum of bourgeois amenities—telephones, heating, "good food," etc.).

Clearly it was an odd position. There was a certain ghostliness, one might very well say, about writing for people who probably wouldn't be interested. And that sense of a flat landscape stretching out forever was heightened by the fact that, as a writer for the theatre I was not joining an artistic community committed to any particular struggle or agenda. The cafés of the Impressionists and the bars of the Abstract Expressionists had no equivalents on the streets I traveled. I didn't live in a world like Renaissance Florence, in which sculptors vied for the honor of putting their particular subtly different vision of a hero or a god in a public square, because as far as I could see there were no types or models toward which I ought to strive, no public squares, and, in a way, no public.

No one would reward me, and no one would punish me, if I followed the conventions of nineteenth-century theatre or rejected them, if I wrote in a more naturalistic style or in a more surrealistic style. In writing a play, should I draw my inspiration from George Balanchine's ballets? Frederick Wiseman's documentaries? The verses of James Merrill, Fra Angelico's frescoes, the songs on the radio, the day's newspaper, my own life? No one cared.

In the corner of the universe where I'd be writing, there'd been a breakdown in the system of rewards and punishments that behaviorists would consider the only possible system for teaching a dog or a writer how to do a task well. And yet the breakdown meant I was totally free.

Well then, what was the outcome? Was the game lost or won? Were the plays worthwhile and valuable, or weren't they? Regrettably, I may never know. Freedom and self-confidence enabled me to write ambitious plays. I amused myself, and then I died, I suppose, with the results of the experiment still undetermined.

Writing about Sex
2008

For whatever reason, and I don't remember how it happened, I am now what people call "sixty-four years old," and I have to admit that I started writing about sex almost as soon as I realized that it was possible to do so—say, at the age of fourteen—and I still do it, even though I was in a way the wrong age then, and in a different way I guess I'm the wrong age now. Various people who have liked me or cared about me—people who have believed in my promise as a writer—have hinted to me at different times in my life that an excessive preoccupation with the subject of sex has harmed or even ruined my writing. They've implied that it was sad, almost pitiful, that an adolescent obsession—or maybe it was in fact a psychological compulsion—should have been allowed to marginalize what they optimistically had hoped might have been a serious body of work. Meanwhile, people I don't know very well have tended over all those decades to break into a very particular smile, one I recognize now, when they've learned that I've written something that deals with sex—a winking smile that seems to suggest that a trivial, silly, but rather amusing topic has been mentioned. It's a smile not unlike the smile that would appear on the faces of some of our more conservative teachers in the 1950s when the topic of "jazz" was raised—a smile sometimes accompanied back in those gloomy days by a mocking, suggestive swaying of the hips.

I suppose it goes without saying that James Joyce, D. H. Lawrence and others were expanding the scope of literature and redrawing humanity's picture of itself when they approached this subject in the earlier part of the twentieth century. But by the time I came along, many of my friends were embarrassed on my behalf precisely because the topic I was writing about seemed so closely associated with an earlier era.

So why have I stuck with it? I suppose it has to do with the point I've heard boringly expressed by writers in one way or another all of my life—the thing they always say, while in a way always hoping that no one will believe them, though what they're saying is true—some variation or another of "I don't do my own writing." I personally sometimes express the point, when pressed, by saying that I see my writing as a sort of collaboration between my rational self ("me") and the voice that comes from outside the window, the voice that comes in through the window, whose words I write down in a state of weirded-out puzzlement, thinking, "Jesus Christ, what is he saying?"

The collaboration is really quite an unequal partnership, I'd have to admit. The voice contributes everything, and I contribute nothing, frankly, except some modest organizing abilities and (if I may say so) a certain skill in finding, among the voice's many utterances, those that are most interesting. (I suppose I'm quite a bit like one of those young college graduates in jacket and tie who helps some unruly but for some reason celebrated man to write his autobiography.) When I try to define the voice, I say, weakly, "Oh, that's the unconscious," but I'm eventually forced to conclude that, if the unconscious has thoughts, it has to have heard these thoughts (or at least their constituent fragments) from human beings of some description—from the people I've met, the people I've read about, the people I've happened to overhear on the street. So it's not just a theory that society is speaking to itself through me. If it were not so, all I would be able to hear, and all I would be trying to transcribe, would be the sound of my own heart sending blood through my veins.

Obviously, society has asked writers, as a group, to take time out from normal labor to do this special listening and transcribing, and each individual writer has been assigned a certain part of the spectrum. No writer knows—or can know—whether the section that's been assigned to him contains the valuable code that will ultimately benefit the human species or whether his section consists merely of the more common noise or chatter. But obviously, the system can only work if everyone dutifully struggles to do his best with the material that's been given to him, rather than trying to do what has already been assigned to somebody else.

The voice outside my own particular window has repeatedly come back to the subject of sex. And sure, I regret it in a way, or it sometimes upsets me. But if I were to conclude that the voice is fundamentally not to be trusted, where would I be then? The enterprise of writing would have to come to an end for me, because on what basis could I possibly decide to reject what the voice was saying so insistently? The truth is that if I tried to listen to somebody else's voice instead of mine, I wouldn't be able to hear it. And without an outside voice, what would I write down? Who would I listen to? "Me"? It doesn't work that way. So at a certain point—and with a certain sadness, because of how I knew I would be seen by other people—I decided I was going to trust the voice I was hearing. And of course, like every writer, I hope I'll be one of the ones who will be led to do something truly worthwhile. But in another way, it actually doesn't matter whether it's me or not. That's just a game—who did the best? The actually important question is not whether "I" am one of the better cogs in the machine—the important question is whether the whole mechanism of which I'm a part is or is not one of evolution's cleverer species-survival devices, one that might be very helpful—even at the last minute.

Why is sex interesting to write about? To some, that might seem like a rather dumb question. Obviously when someone interested in geology is alone in a room, he or she tends to think a lot about rocks. And I imagine that when many geologists were children, they put pictures having to do with rocks on their bedroom walls.

And I would have to guess that geologists find it fun to sit at a desk and write about rocks. So, yes, I find it enjoyable to write about sex. But apart from that, I still find myself wondering, "Why is it interesting to write about sex?"

One reason is that sex is shocking. Yes, it's still shocking, after all these years—isn't that incredible? At least it's shocking to me. And I suppose I think it's shocking because, even after all these years, most bourgeois people, including me, still walk around with an image of themselves in their heads that doesn't include—well—that. I'm vaguely aware that while going about my daily round of behavior, I'm making use of various mammalian processes, such as breathing, digesting, and getting from place to place by hobbling about on those odd legs we have. But the fact is that when I form a picture of myself, I see myself doing the sorts of things that humans do and only humans do—things like hailing a taxi, going to a restaurant, voting for a candidate in an election, or placing receipts in various piles and adding them up. But if I'm unexpectedly reminded that my soul and body are capable of being totally swept up in a pursuit and an activity that pigs, flies, wolves, lions, and tigers also engage in, my normal picture of myself is violently disrupted. In other words, consciously, I'm aware that I'm a product of evolution, and I'm part of nature. But my unconscious mind is still partially wandering somewhere in the early nineteenth century and doesn't know these things yet.

Writing about sex is really a variant of what Wordsworth did, that is, it's a variant of writing about nature, or as we call it now, "the environment." Sex is "the environment" coming inside, coming into our home or apartment and taking root inside our own minds. It comes out of the mud where the earliest creatures swam; it comes up and appears in our brains in the form of feelings and thoughts. It sometimes appears with such great force that it sweeps other feelings and other thoughts completely out of the way. And on a daily basis it quietly and patiently approaches the self and winds itself around it and through it until no part of the self is unconnected to it.

Sex is of course an extraordinary meeting-place of reality and dream, and it's also—what is not perhaps exactly the same thing—an extraordinary meeting-place of the meaningful and the meaningless. The big toe, for example, is one part of the human body, human flesh shaped and constructed in a particular way. The penis is another part of the body, located not too far away from the big toe and built out of fundamentally the same materials. The act of sex, the particular shapes of the penis and the vagina, are the way they are because natural selection has made them that way. There may be an adaptive value to each particular choice that evolution made, but from our point of view as human beings living our lives, the evolutionary explanations are unknown, and the various details present themselves to us as completely arbitrary. It can only be seen as funny that men buy magazines containing pictures of breasts, but not magazines with pictures of knees or forearms. It can only be seen as funny that demagogues give speeches denouncing men who insert their penises into other men's anuses—and then go home to insert their own penises into their wives' vaginas! (One might have thought it obvious that either both of these acts are completely outrageous, or neither of them is.) And yet the interplay and permutations of the apparently meaningless, the desire to penetrate anus or vagina, the glimpse of the naked breast, the hope of sexual intercourse or the failure of it, lead to joy, grief, happiness, or desperation for the human creature.

Perhaps it is the power of sex that has taught us to love the meaningless and thereby turn it into the meaningful. Amazingly, the love of what is arbitrary (which one could alternatively describe as the love of reality) is something we human beings are capable of feeling (and perhaps even what we call the love of the beautiful is simply a particular way of exercising this remarkable ability). So it might not be absurd to say that if you love the body of another person, if you love another person, if you love a meadow, if you love a horse, if you love a painting or a piece of music or the sky at night, then the power of sex is flowing through you.

Yes, some people go through life astounded every day by the beauty of forests and animals; some are astounded more frequently by the beauty of art; and others by the beauty of other human beings. But science could one day discover that the ability to be astounded by the beauty of other human beings came first, and to me it seems implausible to imagine that these different types of astonishment or appreciation are psychologically unrelated.

It's also interesting to write about sex because it's often noted that writers like to write about conflict, and of course conflict is built into the theme of sex. A story about a person who wants to have a plate of spaghetti might be interesting, but a story about a person who wants to have another person—now, that is potentially even more interesting, because the person who is wanted may not want in return. But leaving aside the conflict involved in the fact that people's desires are often at cross purposes, sex often destroys lives and leads to tragedy. Indeed, sex has always been known to be such a powerful force that fragile humanity can't help but be terribly fearful in front of it, and so powerful barriers have been devised to control it—taboos of all varieties, first of all, and then all the emotions subsumed under the concepts of jealousy and possessiveness, possessiveness being a sort of anticipatory form of jealousy. (I noticed recently that a sociological survey of married people in the United States found that when asked the question: "What is very important for a successful marriage?" the quality mentioned most frequently—by 93 percent of the respondents—was "faithfulness," while "happy sexual relationship" came in with only 70 percent. In other words, to 23 percent of the respondents, it seemed more important that they and their partner should not have sex with others than that they themselves should enjoy sex.)

Sex seems capable of creating anarchy, and those who are committed to predictability and order find themselves inevitably either standing in opposition to it, or occasionally trying to pretend to themselves that it doesn't even exist. My local newspaper, the *New York Times*, for example, does not include images of naked people. Many of its readers might enjoy it much much more if it did, but those same readers still might not buy it if those images were in it, because if it contained such images it couldn't present the portrait of a normal, stable, adequate world—a world not ideal, but still good enough—which a great many readers hope to find each day. Nudity somehow seems to imply that anything could happen, but many readers would rather believe that many things will *not* happen, because the world is under control, benevolent people are looking out for us, the situation is not as bad as we tend to think, and while problems do exist, they can be solved by wise rulers. The contemplation of nudity or sex could tend to bring up the alarming idea that at any moment human passions might rise up and topple the world we know.

But perhaps it would be a good thing if people saw themselves as a part of nature, connected to the environment in which they live. Sex can be a very humbling, equalizing force. It's often been noted that naked people do not wear medals, and weapons are forbidden inside the pleasure garden. When the sexuality of the terrifying people we call "our leaders" is for some reason revealed, they lose some of their power—sometimes all of it—because we're reminded (and strangely, we need reminding) that they are merely creatures like the ordinary worm or beetle that creeps along at the edge of the pond. Sex really is a nation of its own. Those whose allegiance is given to sex at a certain moment withdraw their loyalty temporarily from other powers. It's a symbol of the possibility that we might all defect for one reason or another from the obedient columns in which we march.

Why I Call Myself a Socialist
2010

In most reasonably large towns in the United States and Europe, you can find, on some important public square or street, a professional theatre. And so in various quiet neighborhoods in these towns you can usually also find some rather quiet individuals, the actors who work regularly in that theatre, individuals whose daily lives center around lawns and cars and cooking and shopping and occasionally the athletic events of children, but who surprisingly at night put on the robes of kings and wizards, witches and queens, and for their particular community they temporarily embody the darkest needs and loftiest hopes of the human species.

The actor's role in the community is quite unlike anyone else's. Businessmen, for example, don't take their clothes off or cry in front of strangers in the course of their work. Actors do.

Contrary to the popular misconception, the actor is not necessarily a specialist in imitating or portraying what he knows about other people. On the contrary, the actor may simply be a person who's more willing than others to reveal some truths about himself. Interestingly, the actress who, in her own persona, may be gentle, shy, and socially awkward, someone whose hand trembles when pouring a cup of tea for a visiting friend, can convincingly portray an elegant, cruel aristocrat tossing off malicious epigrams in an eighteenth century chocolate house. On stage, her hand doesn't shake when she pours the cup of chocolate, nor does she hesitate when passing along dreadful gossip about her closest friends. The actress's next-door neighbors, who may not have had the chance to see her perform, might say that the person they know could never have been, under any circumstances, either elegant or cruel. But she knows the truth that in fact she could have been either or both, and when she plays her part, she's simply showing the audience what she might have been, if she'd in fact been an aristocrat in a chocolate house in the eighteenth century.

We are not what we seem. We are more than what we seem. The actor knows that. And because the actor knows that hidden inside himself there's a wizard and a king, he also knows that when he's playing himself in his daily life, he's playing a part, he's performing, just as he's performing when he plays a part on stage. He knows that when he's on stage performing, he's in a sense deceiving his friends in the audience less than he does in daily life, not more, because on stage he's disclosing the parts of himself that in daily life he struggles to hide. He knows, in fact, that the role of himself is actually a rather small part, and that when he plays that part he must make an enormous effort to conceal the whole universe of possibilities that exists inside him.

Actors are treated as uncanny beings by non-actors because of the strange voyage into themselves that actors habitually make, traveling outside the small territory of traits that are seen by their daily acquaintances as "them." Actors, in contrast, look at non-actors with a certain bewilderment, and secretly think, "What an odd life those people lead! Doesn't it get a bit—claustrophobic?"

It's commonly noted that we all come into the world naked. And at the beginning of each day, most of us find ourselves naked once again, in that strange suspended moment before we put on our clothes.

In various religions, priests put on their clothes quite solemnly, according to a ritual. Policemen, soldiers, janitors, and hotel maids get up in the morning, get dressed, go to work, go to their locker rooms, remove their clothes, and get dressed again in their respective uniforms. The actor goes to the theatre, goes to his dressing room, and puts on his costume. And as he does so, he remembers the character he's going to play—how the character feels, how the character speaks. The actor, in costume, looks in the mirror, and it all comes back to him.

When the actor steps on to the stage to begin the play, he wants to convince the audience that what they're seeing is not a play, but reality itself. The costume that the actor wears, and the voice, the diction, the accent, the way of speaking that begin to return to the actor when he puts on the costume, are devices designed to set in motion a capacity possessed by every member of the audience, a special human capacity whose existence as part of our genetic makeup is what makes theatre possible—that is, our capacity to believe what we want and need to believe about any person who is not ourself.

Because let's be frank—other people are not me, and people who are not me will always in a way be alien to me, they will always in a way be strangers to me, and I will never know with any certainty what they're like. So yes, it's possible to believe a fantasy about them.

Now, I've never met my own genes or looked at them under a microscope, but nonetheless I feel I can make some guesses about what they're like. One thing I feel I know is that I'm amazingly responsive to visual cues about other people, and I'm prepared to guess that this is characteristic of our entire species. And this is why people who can afford it spend enormous sums of money on haircuts and clothes. And this is why films, which deal in close-ups, pay an enormous amount of attention to makeup and hair. And this is why actors in plays take their costumes very, very seriously. It's all because people really do believe what visual cues say. A haircut can express thoughts on a person's behalf. A haircut can say, "I'm intelligent, disciplined, precise, and dynamic." A different haircut can say, "I'm not very bright, I'm sort of a slob, I don't care what happens to me, I don't care what you think of me." There are haircuts that can say, "I find sex an interesting subject, I'm interested in how I look, I'm rather fun, and I think life is great," and there are haircuts that say, "I'm not interested in sex, and I think life is awful." Clothes work in a different way. While the shape of one's head, as completed by one's hair, describes personality, clothes tell us about a person's role in society. But there's an extraordinary similarity in the speed with which we respond to the cues from haircuts and from clothes and in the strength of our belief that what they're telling us is true. So when the actor comes on stage in the costume of a king, I'm prepared to believe that he is a king.

The actor on stage is living in reality. He knows that there is indeed a king inside him. But he also knows very well that Fate has made him an actor and not actually a king. The audience member looking at the actor on stage steps out of reality and lives in illusion until the curtain comes down.

Our capacity to fantasize about other people and to believe our own fantasies makes it possible for us to enjoy this valuable art form, theatre. But unfortunately it's a capacity which has brought incalculable harm and suffering to human beings.

It's well known what grief and even danger can result when we make use of this capacity in our romantic lives and eagerly ascribe to a potential partner benevolent characteristics which are based on our hopes and not on truth.

And one can hardly begin to describe the anguish caused by our habit of using our fantasizing capacity in the opposite direction, that is, using it to ascribe negative characteristics to people who for one reason or another we'd like to think less of. Sometimes we do this in regard to large groups of people, none of whom we've met. But we can even apply our remarkable capacity in relation to individuals or groups whom we know rather well, sometimes simply to make ourselves feel better about things that we happen to have done to them or are planning to do. You couldn't exactly say, for example, that Thomas Jefferson had no familiarity with dark-skinned people. His problem was that he couldn't figure out how to live the life he in fact was living unless he owned these people as slaves. And as it would have been unbearable to him to see himself as so heartless, unjust, and cruel as to keep in bondage people who were just like himself, he ignored the evidence that was in front of his eyes and clung to the fantasy that people from Africa were not his equals.

Well, one could write an entire political history of the human race by simply recounting the exhausting cycle of fantasies which different groups have believed at different times about different other groups. Of course these fantasies were absurd in every case. After a while one does grasp the pattern: Africans, Jews, Mexicans, same-sex lovers, women. Then, after a certain period of time somebody says, Well, actually, they're not that different from anybody else, they have the same capacities, I don't like all of them, some of them are geniuses, etc. etc. The revelations are always in the same direction. We learn about one group or another the thing that actors quickly learn in relation to themselves when they become actors: people are more than they seem to be. We're all rather good at seeing through last year's fantasies and moving on—and rather proud of it too. "Oh yes, after voting for Barack Obama, we took a marvelous vacation in Vietnam," "We went to a reading of the poetry of Octavio Paz with our friends the Goldsteins, and we saw Ellen DeGeneres and Portia de Rossi there—they looked fantastic"—whatever. It's this year's fantasies that present a difficulty.

Are we more brilliant than Thomas Jefferson? Probably not. So there's our situation: it's delightfully easy to see through illusions held by people far away or by members of one's own group a century ago or a decade ago or a year ago. But this doesn't seem to help us to see through the illusions which at any given moment happen to be shared by the people who surround us, our friends, our family, the people we trust.

Around 400,000 babies are born on earth each day. Some are born irreparably damaged, casualties of the conditions in which their mothers lived—victims of polluted water and mysterious chemicals that sneak into the body and warp the genes. But the much more tragic and more horrible truth is that most of these babies are born healthy. There's nothing wrong with them. Every one of them is ready to develop into a person whose intelligence, insight, aesthetic taste, and love of other people could help to make the world a better place. Every one of them is ready to become a person who wakes up happily in the morning because they know they're going to spend the day doing work they find fascinating, work that they love. They're born with all the genetic gifts they could possibly need. Wiggling beside their mothers, they have no idea what's going to be done to them.

In the old days of the Soviet Five Year Plans, the planners tried to determine what ought to happen to the babies born under their jurisdiction. They would calculate how many managers the economy needed, how many researchers, how many factory workers. And the Soviet leaders would organize society in an attempt to channel the right number of people into each category. In most of the world today, the invisible hand of the global market performs this function.

I've sometimes noted that many people in my generation, born during World War Two, are obsessed, as I am, by the image of the trains arriving at the railroad station at Auschwitz and the way that the S.S. officers who greeted the trains would perform on the spot what was called a "selection," choosing a few of those getting off of each train to be slave laborers, who would get to live for as long as they were needed, while everyone else would be sent to the gas chambers almost immediately. And just as inexorable as were these "selections" are the determinations made by the global market when babies are born. The global market selects out a tiny group of privileged babies who are born in certain parts of certain towns in certain countries, and these babies are allowed to lead privileged lives. Some will be scientists, some will be bankers. Some will command, rule, and grow fantastically rich, and others will become more modestly paid intellectuals or teachers or artists. But all the members of this tiny group will have the chance to develop their minds and realize their talents. As for all the other babies, the market will sort them and stamp labels onto them and hurl them roughly into various pits. If the market thinks that workers will be needed in electronics factories, a few hundred thousand babies will be stamped with the label "factory worker," and each will be assigned a certain appropriate education and a certain appropriate upbringing in a certain appropriate neighborhood, and when the moment comes when the baby is old enough to work, well, a nervous young woman will find herself standing at the gate of a factory in India or in China or in Mexico, and she'll be assigned to a certain workstation where she'll assemble various things for sixteen hours a day, she'll sleep in the factory dormitory, she won't be allowed to speak to her fellow workers, she'll have to ask for permission to go the bathroom, she'll be subjected to the sexual whims of her boss, and she'll be breathing fumes day and night that will make her ill and lead to her death at an early age. And when she has died, one will be able to say about her that she worked, like a nurse, not to benefit herself but to benefit others. Except that a nurse works to benefit the sick, while the factory worker will have worked to benefit the owners of her factory. She will have devoted her hours, her consideration, her energy and strength to increasing their wealth. She will have lived and died for that. And it's not that anyone sadly concluded when she was born that she lacked the talent to become, let's say, a violinist, a conductor, or perhaps another Mozart. The reason she was sent to the factory and not to the concert hall was not that she lacked ability but that the market wanted workers, and so she was one of the ones who was assigned to be one.

And during the period when all the babies who are born have been sorted into their different categories and labeled, during the period when you could say that they're being nourished in their pens until they're ready to go to work, they're all assigned appropriate costumes. And once they know what costume they'll wear, each individual is given an accent, a way of speaking, some characteristic personality traits, and a matching body type, and each person's face starts slowly to specialize in certain expressions which coordinate well with their personality, body type, and costume. And so each person comes to understand what role they will play, and so each can consistently select and reproduce, through all the decades and changes of fashion, the appropriate style and wardrobe, for the rest of their life.

Even those of us who were selected out from the general group have our role and our costume. I happen to play a semi-prosperous fortunate bohemian, not doing too badly, nor too magnificently. And as I walk out onto the street on a sunny day, dressed in my fortunate bohemian costume, I pass, for example, the burly cop on the beat, I pass the weedy professor in his rumpled jacket, distractedly ruminating as he shambles along, I see couples in elegant suits briskly rushing to their meetings, I see the art student and the law student, and in the background, sometimes looming up as they come a bit closer, those not particularly selected out—the drugstore cashier in her oddly-matched pink shirt and green slacks, the wacky street hustler with his crazy dialect and his crazy gestures, the wisecracking truck drivers with their round bellies and leering grins, the grim-faced domestic worker who's slipped out from her employer's house and now races into a shop to do an errand, and I see nothing, I think nothing, I have no reaction to what I'm seeing, because I believe it all. I simply believe it. I believe the costumes. I believe the characters. And then for one instant, as the woman runs into the shop, I suddenly see what's happening, the way a drowning man might have one last vivid glimpse of the glittering shore, and I feel like screaming out, "Stop! Stop! This isn't real! It's all a fantasy! It's all a play! The people in these costumes are not what you think! The accents are fake, the expressions are fake—Don't you see? It's all—" One instant—and then it's gone. My mind goes blank for a moment, and then I'm back to where I was. The domestic worker runs out of the shop and hurries back towards her job, and once again I see her only as the character she plays. I see a person who works as a servant. And surely that person could never have lived, for example, the life I've lived, or been like me—she's not intelligent enough. She had to be a servant. She was born that way. The hustler surely had to be a hustler, it's all he could do, the cashier could never have worn beautiful clothes, she could never have been someone who sought out what was beautiful, she could only ever have worn that pink shirt and those green slacks.

So, just as Thomas Jefferson lived in illusion, because he couldn't face the truth about the slaves that he owned, I too put to use every second of my life, like my beating heart, this capacity to fantasize which we've all been granted as our dubious birthright. My belief in the performance unfolding before me allows me not to remember those dreadful moments when all of those babies were permanently maimed, and I was spared. The world hurled the infant who became the domestic worker to the bottom of a pit and crippled her for life, and I saw it happen, but I can't remember it now. And so now it seems quite wonderful to me that the world today treats the domestic worker and me with scrupulous equality. It seems wonderfully right. If I steal a car, I go to jail, and if she steals a car, she goes to jail. If I drive on the highway, I pay a toll, and if she drives on the highway, she pays a toll. We compete on an equal basis for the things we want. If I apply for a job, I take the test, and if she applies for the job, she takes the test. And I go through my life thinking it's all quite fair.

If we look at reality for more than an instant, if we look at the human beings passing us on the street, it's not bearable. It's not bearable to watch while the talents and the abilities of infants and children are crushed and destroyed. These happen to be things that I just can't think about. And most of the time, the factory workers and domestic workers and cashiers and truck drivers can't think about them either. Their performances as these characters are consistent and convincing, because they actually believe about themselves just what I believe about them, that what they are now is all that they could ever have been, they could never have been anything other than what they are. Of course that's what we all have to believe, so that we can bear our lives and live in peace together. But it's the peace of death.

Actors understand the infinite vastness hiding inside each human being, the characters not played, the characteristics not revealed. Schoolteachers can see every day that, given the chance, the sullen pupil in the back row can sing, dance, juggle, do mathematics, paint, and think. If the play we're watching is an illusion, if the baby who now wears the costume of the hustler in fact had the capacity to become a biologist or a doctor, a circus performer or a poet or a scholar of Ancient Greek, then the division of labor, as now practiced, is inherently immoral, and we must somehow learn a different way to share out all the work that needs to be done. The costumes are wrong. They have to be discarded. We have to start out naked again and go from there.

Night Thoughts
2017

Murder

Night. A hotel. A dark room on a high floor. Outside the hotel, miles of empty city streets, silent and gray. A few desperate people wandering. Rather cold. I turn on a dim lamp and stare at the newspaper, and my eye goes as always to the stories about crime, the murders. A crime of passion—jealousy, frenzy—a body falling in the shower. Strange deaths in a quiet suburb—an odd weapon—a serial killer? My senses quicken, my lethargy falls away. They're writing about me. Well, no, not me, not quite, not yet. But I know, as I read, that I'm not reading as the victim, I'm reading as the murderer.

In a courtroom, the case of a robbery gone wrong. The thief had been inside the house when the man who owned it unexpectedly came home. The thief had gone after the man with a knife, and when he was asked, "Why did you stab him thirty-eight times when you knew he was dead after the first blow?" the murderer's answer was, "I don't know." Murderers always seem to say, "I don't know"—unless they say, "I can't remember what happened."

Then, on the television, a different kind of murder. Brightly dressed university students in pools of blood, their books scattered all over the street. The Islamic State. A machine gun. Screaming. Sobbing. An Arab empire in the fourteenth century?

In this dead, ruined neighborhood—all shards and scraps floating in the wind—the hotel itself is rather magnificent, resplendent with ballrooms, as if we were living in the nineteenth century. Not long before, some young people from a housing project in the neighborhood had put together quite a lot of money in order to put on tuxedos and evening gowns and hold a celebration in one of the ballrooms. As the party wore on, one boy thought another boy had flirted with his date. A fight broke out. Mayhem in the ballroom. Then shots were fired, and the party ended in bondage and death—one boy gone forever, another boy handcuffed and carried away.

NIGHT

The television screen keeps turning back obsessively, crazily, to the face of Donald Trump. Oh my God—will this never end? I turn off the television, turn out the light. When I try to fall asleep, Trump keeps jumping back at me, then he slowly fades out, and I think about myself, the course of my life.

Good luck from the beginning. People were paid to take care of me. We lived in a large apartment building in a very big city, and if my mother wanted something heavy to be moved from one room to another, or if she thought the dishwasher was making a peculiar sound, she would call the building superintendent, and someone would appear to fix the problem. Books and music from the very beginning.

Books and music. Nobody ever exactly said this to me, but I took it as implied: what I was going to do in the life ahead of me was to try to be happy. That was going to be my principal professional responsibility. I would wake up every day and try to become happier.

I remember a thin, wispy-haired man holding a long cigarette in my parents' living room, talking about Beethoven . . .

For various reasons, my friends and I all turned out to be, to varying degrees, what people decades ago used to call "downward mobile." Our positions in society are somewhat lower than the ones our parents held. During the years when I was growing up, my father never went to a grocery store to buy food. Other people did that for him. He never walked home from the grocery store carrying a bag of groceries. He never walked up flights of stairs to his apartment while carrying his groceries. I do those things. I live in a small building, and if there's a problem with the electricity or the plumbing, I can't ask a building superintendent to send someone over to fix it. All the same, my luck has held. I live in a quiet, tranquil part of town. I write. I read. I visit friends. I go to concerts. I go to restaurants.

When I was twenty, I learned about the lives people led in the imperial Japanese court in the eleventh century. It was all described in the novel *The Tale of Genji* by Lady Murasaki Shikibu and *The Pillow Book* of Sei Shonagon, which was a sort of diary or journal. I could tell right away that this was the sort of life that was appropriate for me—women and men who had nothing to do all day but speculate and talk about love and beauty. Or so it seemed. Reclining on pillows next to each other, they wrote letters and poems from early in the morning till late at night, on perfumed paper of many different colors. It seemed like a life to aspire to, anyway.

ANXIETIES

Obviously I'm upset about what my species has turned out to be—the species that went mad and destroyed the planet. It's unbelievable to recall how respected and admired the human animal was at one time. It's as if the old family dog, once universally beloved, had suddenly become rabid, his muzzle now covered with foam, his presence terrifying. And of course I'm upset about—why should I deny it?—I'm very upset about the Islamic State, about all the various factions and groups that branched off from Al Qaeda, the disciples of bin Laden, the crazy bin Ladenists. I'm frightened of all the things they might decide to do to us, the dirty bombs, the poison gas. Sometimes I wonder, did this individual person, Osama bin Laden, really have anything to do with that horrible day in 2001? Did he really plan the attack, or did we just choose him to be the personification of it? Who knows? Most of the evidence about the attack seems to come from people who were tortured—how can you believe it? But everyone agrees that bin Laden was pleased about what happened on that day. Anyway, we made him the symbol of it. Someone had to be. And so he had to be killed, obviously. Now his followers are stronger than ever, and it's awful, it's sickening, to know that there are these people out there in the world who would like to hurt me, who would like to eliminate me, whether they're standing next to me in a line at the airport or plotting secretly in a desert in Yemen. It's a terrible thought.

I'm also upset about "morality," not a word you hear much in conversation, really, but both my parents and my teachers in school were great devotees of it. They loved morality. I sometimes ask myself, What strange demon would have created an animal that could say to itself, "I'm doing this, and I want to do it, and I'm glad I'm doing it, but I shouldn't be doing it, because it's not 'right,' it's 'wrong.'" It's so peculiar. "Right" and "wrong" were like two little chimes that were constantly being struck in my parents' apartment. And as I go about my life, the chimes are still being struck inside my head, and I sometimes wonder—chime—if something about the way I live—chime—might somehow be "wrong"—chime chime.

CIVILIZATION

When I was in my late twenties, I visited a small, dark apartment in a bohemian section of town, and it was much rougher than the apartments my friends and I had grown up in. The tiny sink in the bathroom looked like it hadn't even been installed by a professional plumber. I was frightened by the smallness and the darkness of the apartment, and when I first walked into it I felt very ill at ease, but after a while the place began to seem rather warm and cozy, and I started to feel quite comfortable there, perhaps more comfortable than I'd ever felt in any other place, because I was drawn to the mysterious, alluring woman who lived in the apartment. She apparently didn't mind that the apartment was so small and dark—she seemed to think it wasn't really that bad. She could read there. She could even cook there—and she cooked quite a number of very delicious things. She could listen to music there—she had quite a few records—but at a certain moment she shocked me by saying that she thought civilization might have been a mistake, a mistake from the beginning. Excuse me?—my God—that was such an unsettling thing to say. It really disturbed me. I got very upset and couldn't understand what in the world she meant. Civilization? Civilization could only be good, from my point of view. Without civilization—well—all the things I cared about—and actually, all the things she seemed to care about too—they wouldn't have existed—no books, no music, no bohemian section of the city, no city at all. She'd come to the city to find a kind of freedom that couldn't have existed without civilization. Even the relationship we were about to embark on couldn't have existed without civilization.

And I could still remember the vivid images that had formed in my mind when I was a very young boy, and one of my teachers had spoken of the magnificent loam that had been created when the Nile overflowed its banks. So much that was glorious had grown out of the fertility of that extraordinary loam—pyramids, paintings, astonishing sculptures . . . And I remembered the phrase, "Civilization means specialization." The brilliant idea that the sandal-maker wouldn't need to grow food, because he could get his food from the farmer in exchange for sandals, and the pharaoh didn't need to grow food or make sandals because the farmer and the sandal-maker paid taxes to the pharaoh so he could be the pharaoh and buy food and sandals and hire painters and sculptors. Incredibly clever. And I remembered, from my parents' living room, full of ashtrays and whiskey, that that thin old wispy-haired man had said something to the effect that all of civilization was justified by the fact that it finally produced Beethoven, the beauty of whose work was a kind of absolute—unanswerable and undeniable. And yet what the woman in the apartment had said stayed with me for weeks, then for years. It stayed with me and upset me, and I kept thinking about it. And about two decades later she stood beside me in a square in East Berlin as we read Brecht's poem carved in stone:

Wer baute das siebentorige Theben?
In den Büchern stehen die Namen von Königen.
Haben die Königen die Felsenbrocken herbeigeschleppt? . . .

Who built Thebes with its seven gates?
In books, we're given the names of kings.
Did the kings carry on their own backs those massive fragments of stone? . . .

In his sixteen-line poem, Brecht quarreled with "the books." "The books" talked about the kings. The books Brecht had read, and the books I had read, praised the kings for the fantastic cities they'd built, the fantastic cities with their gates and their towers and their arches. For the writers of books and the readers of books, civilization was great. How fabulous to stand before these wondrous feats of construction and design! But it was a lie to say that the kings built the cities. They didn't build them. And for the peasants and slaves and prisoners of war who actually built them, civilization might not have been great.

As more and more years of my own life followed on and on, I started to be able to see the past in the present, right in front of me, always more clearly—the "story of civilization." The story of civilization was repeated in front of me every day. I'd seen it even in childhood—we all had—the horrors of the playground, the horrors of the schoolyard. The bigger, stronger kid—the kid with the luck to have a little extra strength—could make the weaker kid do what he wanted him to do: The candy bar was handed over, and nothing really could be done about it. We learned the simple lesson: strong triumphs over weak—among lions, among elks, among boys and girls. Men pin women to the ground—and right then they begin to believe that women are inferior—intellectually inferior, humanly inferior. The people with the guns learn that they can easily defeat the people with the spears, and they begin to say that people so easily defeated are "savages," ignorant, and deserve to be slaves.

For the lucky ones on the banks of the Nile, the lucky ones who were right there in the right place at the right time when the river overflowed, it was all fantastic. Fertile land. More could be grown than they even needed—a surplus! How amazing! So, should the surplus be shared with the less lucky people who lived farther from the river and had less fertile soil? No! We won't share it, and in fact we'll use some of it to feed an army to defend us in case anyone doesn't agree with our plan to keep all the surplus for ourselves. And so the lucky people with the surplus passed it all on to their children, their friends, the children of their friends. Once all of that had happened, well, actually making use of the people who lived farther from the river was almost an afterthought. Let's put them to work. Why shouldn't we? Get them to till the fields, and if they also produce a surplus, we'll take that too. And after that, why, they'll be some of the ones who will carry on their backs the massive fragments of stone, carry them and push them all the way up, up, to the top of the pyramid—cities, gates, statues, temples, palaces. And we'll have to recognize that those who are reduced to doing all this agonizing work must obviously be made of inferior clay—if they weren't, they wouldn't have allowed anyone to do to them what we've done to them. And if we do have more than these sad, pitiful people, if we have an advantage, why shouldn't we use it? Why not leverage our advantage to get still more? Do you have five times more than that other guy? Why not ten times more? Why not a hundred times more? For the lucky people, civilization just got more and more fun.

And the process has never stopped. And so the lucky people either have more—or they have much more—or they have much, much more—because a person can be lucky, or very lucky, or very, very lucky—and of course lucky people can also be rapacious, or they can be very rapacious, or they can be very, very rapacious. And the jobs that lucky people have are different from the jobs that unlucky people have. Lucky people give orders. Unlucky people obey orders. Lucky people may actually love their jobs. Their jobs can be lively, their jobs can be thrilling. When they go to work, lucky people are treated with respect. Because lucky people respect each other, and everyone else respects them too. But many unlucky people aren't treated with respect, because lucky people, if they want to, can treat them with contempt. And even if the lucky people don't want to treat them with contempt, can they really respect them? No, not really. How could they really respect people whom they know they could so easily treat with contempt?

There are lucky countries, too, and unlucky countries. If you're an unlucky person, and you're working in, let's say, the United States, and your supervisor doesn't think you work fast enough, or he thinks you ask to go to the bathroom too frequently, he can yell at you or make you work on the late night shift; if you're an unlucky person, and you're working in, let's say, Bangladesh, and your supervisor doesn't like your attitude, he can hit you; and if you're an unlucky person, and you're working in, let's say, Colombia, and your supervisor thinks you're a rebel or a troublemaker, he can say a word to some local goons, and he can have you killed.

Lucky people tend to expand to fill the space their luck has given them. In the city where I live, for example, if you go into any expensive restaurant, you'll quickly learn that very lucky people are often very loud. In those expensive restaurants, the very lucky feel at home, they feel free, they talk very loudly, and sometimes their laughter seems to come up so naturally from the very depth of their bodies that every part of their bodies vibrates and resonates, and their exploding laughter fills the whole room. Unlucky people are often silent. If they're slapped, they're silent. If they're punched, they're silent. If they're shot, they're silent. But every once in a while in certain places, certain moments occur in which the lives of the unlucky have become so painful, so intolerable, that they suddenly look at the lucky people in a very different way, a very strange way, and they suddenly become aware that a terrible injustice has been perpetrated on them, and they cry out, a strange sort of cry of anguish and rage. Unexpectedly, abruptly, there are suddenly riots in certain cities. Cars are overturned. Plate-glass windows are shattered. Indentured farmers burn down the mansion of the landlord. Huge bands of people run out of their houses and try to storm the palace of the ruler.

TEACHERS

In my early years, the very liberal private schools I attended employed quite a number of unusual teachers, teachers whose approach to life might often have seemed to be at cross-purposes with what one might have assumed to be the attitudes of most of the parents whose children were their pupils. The children's fathers were doctors, lawyers, a few were bankers, and most of them had reached those relatively privileged roles in society through steely ambition and competitive struggle. Yet many of these teachers—not all, of course, because we did have a few who were quite old-fashioned—many of these teachers, one would have to say, were rather decadent characters, rather surprising men and women who despised the generally applauded virtues of heroism, manliness, and devotion to "the group." They didn't seem very loyal to any particular team or country, and they didn't seem to approve of the idea that individuals ought to struggle to achieve supremacy. Instead of encouraging competition, they told us quite openly that they didn't believe in it. And the example many of them set us was one of languid self-indulgence and unembarrassed pleasure-seeking. Some of them devoted their lives to art. None of them devoted their lives to making money, and as far as we could tell, none of them had any.

CIVILIZATION

Not long ago I visited some wealthy friends, a young husband and wife who'd employed the same housekeeper for many years. The housekeeper was a warm, friendly, very sensible woman. She took care of the children, did some cleaning and cooking, and I too had known her for quite a while and always called her by her first name. She had worked for the husband before he was married, and when she and the husband chatted and joked together, I could see all the husband's customary tension falling away. He basked in the affection and the intimacy of this relationship they had. It was easy for him, because he knew where he stood; the relationship's terms had been settled long ago. They proceeded from one day to the next on the basis that, after all, he was a superior being, and so, that being the standing assumption, they both behaved in an appropriate style, he with gentle goodwill toward her, she with a kind of amused, informal, joshing deference toward him. And at a certain point during my visit, she knelt down to pick up the toys that the children had left under the dining room table, and I suddenly imagined that she was throwing the toys with all of her might into the husband's face, blinding him, and then that she was smashing his head into the corner of the marble tabletop with overpowering force two or three times until he was dead.

Well, such things don't really happen—do they? Of course the housekeeper knows that only bad consequences would follow if she should murder her employer. And of course most of the time she actually believes that he's a superior being, and so there isn't anything objectionable about the simple fact that he has a superior position in the world, and there's no particular reason to think about murdering him. And it does seem to be the case that he is superior. After all, if he weren't superior, why would he be the employer and she the housekeeper? If he weren't superior, why would she be working for him six days a week, doing all the things he asks her to do? If he weren't superior, why wouldn't he occasionally be working for her? Obviously, that never happens. Every day they play the same parts, and even after years, there's never been a single day on which she gave the orders, and he obeyed them, and so it seems awfully clear that he must be superior. And what does he himself think? Well, he's much too refined to say this out loud, but yes, he secretly thinks that he does possess some special hidden merit, something deep inside him that does make him superior, something perhaps reflected in his way of speaking, his accent, the fact that he excelled in certain subjects at school, his ability to work so seriously at his desk—and he has a good idea of how a superior person would walk and dress and behave, and so he acts that way, he actually impersonates a superior being every moment of his waking life. But of course, at the same time, he's well aware that he's a total fake—he's a fraud—an imposter. What can one say? One has to marvel at the amazing ability of the human mind to accept and contain at the same time two entirely contradictory propositions. Because the remarkable fact is that she also is not at all stupid, and she also knows that the game the two of them play every day is completely insane, she also knows that of course he's not really superior, and she's not really inferior, it's just that he's had much, much better luck—he was given some opportunities, and he took advantage of them.

She knows he's an imposter—and that's a very scary thought, and she knows she has to try not to think it, because if she actually thought it for too long, she might want to kill him, which is exactly what she doesn't want to do. She knows very well that the way to find happiness in this world is not to hate your life but to somehow learn how to accept your life. Take pride in your work, whatever it is. Derive whatever pleasure you can from whatever surrounds you—the sky, the people you like, the light falling on the brick wall.

Morality

But I've actually lived long enough now to have figured out what the word "morality" really refers to. I do know what it means, although it's pretty outrageous. It refers to a very simple thought: we shouldn't accept this principle that strong inevitably triumphs over weak. Luck has distributed strength in an arbitrary way: this lion is stronger, this elk is stronger, this group of people lives closer to the river, this group of people lives farther away. Luck has given the person with the penis, the people with the guns, a bit more strength, and so they've trampled over everyone else. Morality says we shouldn't accept that. For the bigger kid to take the smaller kid's candy bar is not right; it's wrong. And if the bigger kid gives that candy bar to me, the process by which I received it was wrong, and it's wrong for me to have it, and it's wrong for me to eat it.

A Cry

Today a cry of anguish and rage is rising into the air from some of the followers of the religion of Islam. And we're totally shocked! It was surprising enough when strangely dressed religious leaders took over the government of such a large country as Iran. But now, these bin Ladenists!? The tactics they've used are bloodthirsty, sadistic. They shamelessly show their pleasure when their enemies are killed. They touch their victims, they look at their faces. They film the killings! These are all things that we would never do—well, except on very rare occasions, like the time when we killed bin Laden himself. And the reasons they give for their anger seem odd, because their language is religious. A rather large number of people in the West could understand—and many could respect, and quite a few could even deeply admire—the Marxist rebels in Southeast Asia or Latin America who fought so bravely against the ruthless dictators and elites installed in power by the United States. Those who rebel today under the bin Ladenist flag are much, much harder to sympathize with.

But we need to remember that the Western powers, with their enormous fleets of airplanes and ships, have over the decades and centuries forced into a degrading subjugation virtually all the lands where Islam is practiced and immense Islamic empires once ruled. Places whose political, economic, and intellectual influence had once reached across the globe have been forced to submit to the military might of foreign conquerors, and dignified people have been compelled to stand by helplessly as their lands were demeaningly carved into pieces and given new names by alien overlords. And we should accept the fact that, even though Osama bin Laden happened to have been rich, the bin Ladenist movement is a movement of the poor. Almost all of his followers, and the followers of his followers, have been very poor and very unlucky people, just like the followers of the Marxist revolutionaries, and the movement would not exist at all if it didn't express the desperation of these particular people. Some of the members and supporters of the bin Ladenist movement are middle-class or upper-class individuals, just as there have always been middle-class and upper-class participants in virtually all movements of the poor, because there have always been certain members of the privileged classes who, for whatever reason (in Osama bin Laden's case, perhaps partly because his family was recently poor), have sympathized with, and identified with, very poor people.

To eat bad food when you know that others eat good food, to not have food, to be responsible for children and not be able to feed them well, to be sick and know that other people can see a doctor, but you and your family have no doctor you can see, to live surrounded by dirt, to live in ugly rooms in ugly buildings, to know that you can easily be robbed of everything you have, to live in fear of being beaten up, to live in fear of being raped, to live in fear that you or your loved ones could be hurt or killed by people whose authority you cannot challenge—well, yes, poverty is a filthy condition. And when desperate people cry out and risk their lives to say that their condition is awful, one might possibly question the particular points they make in analyzing their situation, but the thing they're saying is basically always true. What they're saying is not wrong. They may be wrong about what caused their condition, they may be wrong about what will cure their condition, but people who cry out—or even do terrible things—because they're in a state of desperation about the circumstances they live in are not deluded. The boy at the party in the hotel ballroom thought his problem was that there was another boy who was flirting with his date. That wasn't his problem. His problem was bad schools, bad health, bad prenatal care, bad childhood nutrition, danger, terror, daily harassment, condescension expressed by authorities who underestimated his intelligence, the fact that in the building he lived in, the garbage was collected on an irregular schedule, the elevator was broken, the lightbulbs in the hallways and the stairwells were broken. The boy's action, the murder, was a form of speech; he was trying to say something.

But, of course, we're puzzled or sometimes almost incredulous when followers of Islam are rioting in the streets or even occasionally killing people because of what we might see as one or another not terribly egregious insult to their religion: in a prison located thousands of miles away from them, a copy of the Koran has been thrown onto the ground, or kicked, or burned. But when people have no control over their own lives, and no feeling of safety, and they don't know how to find the few basic things they need in order to survive, it's not surprising that they hold on tight to their religion—it may be the only thing they have left, and they're afraid that even that might somehow be taken away from them. We can't be surprised by the fact that they adore their religion.

Religion can mean solace and serenity, a kind of security, a private small garden of kindness in a desert of cruelty that seems to stretch out as far as they can see. For people who love the book, for whom the Koran is the fountain that provides the world's only goodness, an insult to the book can feel more painful than blows that are inflicted on their own bodies.

A STORM

And then a couple of decades after our visit to East Berlin, it was an autumn evening, and we were about to have dinner in our lovely apartment, which has large windows looking out on a broad street a couple of blocks away from a very large river. There was a big storm outside, some noisy rain, and all of a sudden the lights in our apartment went out. We'd been through a couple of brief urban blackouts in recent decades, and they always seemed a bit funny, as if we were living in some distant village on a mountaintop, and so we brought out some particularly nice candles and lit them, and I stood in the kitchen in a rather cheerful mood as some sausages quietly fried on the stove, and then we heard weird sounds, a loud honking of cars, and we ran back to our windows and saw something impossible—it was the large river coming down the street, effortlessly crashing into people's basements and pouring inside. And at first I was fascinated and exhilarated by the power of the storm, the magnificence of nature breaking out of its bounds. But by the next morning, when I began to realize that the electricity was not going to be quickly coming back on, and there would be no running water and no heat coming up the pipes, and no one was going to come over and fix things for us, I experienced a feeling of disorientation, as if a lifetime's worth of assumptions were uncontrollably unspooling, and I began to fall into a bizarre state of depression that was unprecedented for me. My sense of humor dropped down, down, all the way to zero. I sat on the bed for hours in the darkness, not moving, not being able to believe how low I had sunk in such a short time as the temperature inside continued to drop.

By the time I had lived long enough to seriously understand what had been explained to me about civilization in that small apartment so many years before, by the time I had seen enough examples of the "story of civilization"—the endlessly repeating story of a strong person holding some squirming weak person's head under the water—seen it enough to really get the message—the vast machinery of civilization itself seemed to be stretching, weakening, and pulling apart . . .

BIN LADENISTS

In an incomprehensible development that caused confused hurt feelings among people in the West, many young Muslims living in the slums of British and European cities were beginning to experience what one could possibly call the pain of the amputated limbs of the Islamic world. These young people had been born in the West but were living with parents and grandparents who had grown up in colonized countries as colonial subjects. Now grandparents, parents, and children were all trying to make a life in the lands of the former colonizers, and it wasn't easy. The young people had to take on the burden of the complex emotions of their parents and grandparents, the conscious anger built up over a lifetime and the unconscious anger built up over a lifetime, as well as dealing with their own personal struggles, and at the same time they were constantly watching images on television and the internet of the countries their families had come from, and the people whose images they were looking at were constantly being blown to pieces all over again by Western invaders. And rather magically or uncannily, many of these young British and European Muslims found that they were suddenly feeling, as if it were their own, the suffering of fellow Muslims in Gaza or Iraq or Syria or Afghanistan, and, seized by a desire to finally put an end to the era of Islamic humiliation at the hands of the West, a few of these young people actually wanted to fly to the Middle East and join the bin Ladenists. This caused audible murmurs in the councils of the lucky, who apparently had no sooner overcome the challenge to their position posed by the atheistic voices of the revolutionary Marxists than they found themselves challenged once again from a different direction by the religious voices of the bin Ladenists.

In England, the Conservative prime minister David Cameron threw himself with abandon into a passionate struggle over young Muslim brains. This earnest man, who was not himself a believer in Islam, and who may or may not have known a lot about Islam, and who—well—quite possibly couldn't have cared less about Islam or any possible interpretation of Islam, nonetheless desperately hoped to find teachers of Islam whose interpretation of the Islamic texts would coincide properly with his own ideas about how Muslims in Britain ought to feel and behave. His benign hope that young Muslims would come to be inspired by a Cameron-friendly type of Islam was then backed up by a program of monitoring, in which ordinary teachers of mathematics or English in British schools were required to make reports to higher authorities if indications appeared that any of the brains in their classrooms were starting to mutate in the wrong direction.

I recalled the one very puritanical teacher I'd had at my school when I was eleven or twelve—her classroom was right next door to the classroom of an elderly woman who was rumored to be a nudist on weekends—and this puritanical teacher was very concerned that we, her pupils, thought too much about sex and had even brought to school certain magazines about sex that contained nude pictures, and so she tried to interest us in different magazines that dealt with what people at that time called "current events"—"international affairs," what was happening in the world. But in David Cameron's classrooms, the teachers became concerned if the students started thinking too little about sex. The teachers were on notice that if students started to dress more conservatively or behave more decorously, if they lost interest in gossiping and started to pray more frequently, if they stopped going to parties and began to read magazines about international affairs, then the higher officials at their schools had to be quietly notified. More importantly, if the children started to believe that Britain and the United States had invaded Iraq in 2003, or that hundreds of thousands of Iraqis had died as a result, then they became potential candidates for thought-retraining programs in which they could relearn how to forget that these things had happened, or relearn how not to care that they had happened, or relearn how not to be upset that they had happened. And if the children began to feel that as Muslims they were looked down upon and discriminated against, that politicians were making hostile statements about them, that their employment prospects were poor, or that they lived in slums, then law enforcement had to be quietly alerted, names taken down, and more serious surveillance seriously considered.

Across the English Channel, a more openly anti-religious campaign is still in progress, because many French politicians and many French intellectuals (still at war, as it seems that they are, with the Catholic Church) seem to be not at all shy about denouncing religion itself—religion in general and Islam in particular. As everyone knows, French lawmakers have promulgated the remarkable rule that young Muslim women are not allowed to wear headscarves in school. In other words, if they want an education, young Muslim women are obliged to violate what some of them consider a tenet of their faith, and they're obliged to appear in public dressed in a way that many of them see as unacceptably immodest, as if Christian girls had to go to school topless. One recent French commentary on bin Ladenist violence in France suggested that the French themselves ought properly to be blamed for it, because French people, according to the commentary, have refused to speak out in their daily lives against the Islamic religion and its various customs. If a Muslim happened to own the sandwich shop on the corner, and the Muslim shop owner declined to sell sandwiches containing pork—this was one example given—then, in the opinion of this commentary, the non-Muslim customer who had wanted such a sandwich ought to openly complain to the shop owner about the ridiculous characteristics of the Islamic religion, rather than meekly looking for his ham sandwich in a different shop. This same attitude of refusing to be sensitive to other people's religious beliefs has led some French intellectuals to defend or even applaud the famous Danish cartoons depicting and mocking Muhammad, along with various similar French cartoons, even though many Muslims believe that the image of the Prophet should not be drawn at all, and even though it clearly causes pain to a large group of individuals to see the person they love and revere being treated disrespectfully, particularly when the disrespect shown to the Prophet runs parallel in their own lives to the disrespect shown every day toward them.

Although it might seem to be clear that what the world needs at the moment is more sensitivity, rather than less, and what French Muslims need is less humiliation, rather than more, the doggedly enthusiastic French proponents of mockery and their various supporters in other Western countries, whenever they're asked what benefit their cartoons and their joking bring to the planet, repeatedly speak of the universal right to freedom of speech and claim that those who dislike their brand of humor want to restrict people's right to say what they like—to which it could certainly in turn be objected that to defend everyone's right to say what they like may be quite appropriate but doesn't remotely require anyone to have any respect or regard or admiration at all for all the vicious, unkind, cruel, horrible, and disgusting things that certain people enjoy saying to hurt other people—and that certain other people enjoy saying to disparage unpopular non-majority groups—denigrating such groups being a delightful, historically popular sport, known to have an important role in the creation of social prejudice, hate, pogroms, lynchings, and genocide.

In contrast to the views of British and French officials, various officials in the government of the United States have a much simpler, two-point solution to the problem of bin Ladenism—point one being, if you see any bin Ladenists living nearby in your own country, lock them up and throw away the key; point two being, in any country that can't prevent you from doing it, kill all the bin Ladenists using bombs and drones.

But the truth is that none of these various approaches to fighting bin Ladenism will actually work. The British approach of trying to indoctrinate and monitor furiously angry people in the hope that they'll adopt a moderate view of life won't work. The French approach of denouncing people's religious beliefs or forcing them to violate some of their religious principles won't work. And the American approach of putting people into prison or killing them most certainly won't work. People who already feel intolerably restricted will only grow angrier when placed in prisons, and the policy of going to different countries and trying to kill all the bin Ladenists, whether by bombing them in large numbers or by firing specialized missiles at them in small groups or one by one, has mysteriously encouraged the growth of bin Ladenism in country after country, because virtually all the bin Ladenists being killed on the ground (not to mention the children, neighbors, and others being killed because they were too close by when the bombs went off) are desperate, poor, very unlucky people, and when the world's most insanely rich and luckiest people start to send bombs into the villages, homes, schools, hospitals, funerals, and wedding parties of people who already are and always have been horribly unlucky, this is so nauseating that great numbers of other unlucky people—those nearby and even those far away from all over the world—will rush to stand by the side of the unlucky victims.

The truth is that once unlucky people come to understand how unlucky they are, it's too late for the lucky. That knowledge cannot be unlearned. Once the right of the lucky to dominate the world has been questioned, the lucky are in trouble. The weird specter of "right" and "wrong" has risen up off the ground and can't be contained.

As long as the world is divided into two groups, those who are lucky and exploit others, and those who are unlucky and are exploited by the lucky, there will always come a moment in one place or another when one of the unlucky people is going to say, "Wait—this is wrong." Of course human beings are articulate creatures, so people who are angry are going to find words to express their anger, whether those words are Marxist words, bin Ladenist words, or any other sort of words. Admittedly, it would be hard to deny that the lucky in the West had quite a lot of success in trying to wipe Marxist words and Marxist ideas off the face of the earth by using the technique of killing Marxists. Indeed, you could make the case that in certain places in the world, unlucky people turned to religious teachers for inspiration and guidance precisely because so many of those who provided inspiration and guidance from a Marxist perspective were dead. You could even say that because of the killing of Marxists by the Western powers, there are places in the world in which the thoughtful, compassionate ideas of Marx were directly replaced by the cruel, reductive ideas of Osama bin Laden. But the unavoidable reality is that even if all the Marxists and all the bin Ladenists were to be safely dead, and all the words they used were to be completely forgotten, so long as the subjugation of unlucky people continued, new words would be found. The feeling of "right and wrong" seems to be somehow innate; it's un-expungeable.

Inspiring and noble groups and individuals have fought against the oppression of the unlucky, and there have also been groups and individuals who were involved in the same struggle who were not inspiring. The bin Ladenists are not inspiring; perhaps they are a manifestation of a sort of frustration or despair that's unusual even among organized groups of tormented people. All the same, one has to recognize that they represent the flamboyant edge, at this particular moment, of the same movement that Marx joined in the nineteenth century and that traces its mostly unwritten history back to the day the first exhausted and broken worker carrying massive fragments of stone up a pyramid turned to a fellow worker and quietly asked the question, "Is there any way to get out of this?"

It's a question that could be asked at any moment by many billions of people who live on our planet.

Upheaval

It has always been wrong that so many unlucky people have been compelled to devote their entire lives to increasing the wealth and the glory of their various lucky masters. And in many places and times, unlucky people have realized that it was within their power to withhold their labor and stop the machine, or even to break the machine and kill the owners of the machine.

But the price unlucky people have paid for doing such things has often been death. Today, though, two developments in particular suggest that a serious upheaval, a change from "below," a change led by the unlucky, a change in how the world is organized, could be more of a possibility than it once was. The first is that worldwide communication between unlucky people is now possible. The second is that the people who now dominate the planet, and the institutions they control, depend on a certain predictability in the behavior of the planet itself. If rivers flow down city streets, and the environment that nurtures us continues to collapse, dramatic shifts in the world's allocation of economic and political power might very well occur.

In any case, under almost any plausible scenario, whatever happens to the world's unlucky people, the life of the lucky is going to change. And when I refer to "the lucky," I don't just mean the very, very lucky billionaires. The lucky people of the world, as I would see it, are a much larger group. In other words, if the city where you live has not been bombed, if your loved ones have not been raped, tortured, or killed, if you've never been harassed or beaten by the police, if you're not afraid to walk after dark in your own neighborhood, if you live in a house or an apartment which is not unbearably cold in the winter or unbearably hot in the summer, if you eat two or three fairly healthy meals a day, and if you're not regularly shouted at or threatened or punished by your boss or manager at work, then you would count as a lucky person, and so that would include, for example, a very large number of the citizens of the United States and Great Britain and most European countries. Those citizens are plausibly to be counted among the lucky because, whether they know it or not, their relatively comfortable lives are made possible by the twist of luck that arranged for them to be born in prosperous countries, and the prosperity of their countries derives in large part from the unjust exploitation of various unlucky human beings, some still living and some now dead.

The United States, for example, has been engaged since 1945 in an extraordinarily audacious attempt to use its diplomatic abilities, its skill at trickery and deceit, and most of all its military power, to place the government of basically every other country on earth at a relative disadvantage; it's an attempt that obviously has had good years and bad years but that on the whole has been surprisingly successful. The purpose of this amazing project has simply been to preserve an international status quo, an international balance of power, which allows a lot of Americans to remain rich. Many individual Americans have opposed some of the more brutal and horrible regimes that their government has succeeded in imposing on certain unlucky nations, and they have spoken, written, and marched in opposition to many of the wars and campaigns of the US government, and they have voted against political candidates whose policies they found particularly heartless and militaristic. Nonetheless, even these dissenting individuals have probably benefited personally, in their material lives, from the great prosperity of their country, a prosperity which would not exist were it not for the powerful international position of the United States. Certain particular policies of the US government have undoubtedly been self-defeating and in their own terms counterproductive and have served to weaken rather than strengthen the position of the United States, but it would be foolish for any American to declare with any degree of certainty—if the clothes they're wearing are comfortable and clean, if they can travel to a different city or a different country on a family vacation, if they can go to the movies or eat in restaurants—that the brutal policies of the United States, financed by the taxes they've paid, have not played a role in allowing them to enjoy those comforts. And of course the exploitation that brings prosperity to the prosperous goes far back into the past as well. The people of Great Britain and Europe are still benefiting today from the exploitation of colonized peoples in the nineteenth century, and the people who live in the United States today are still benefiting from the exploitation of nineteenth century enslaved people in the South whose unpaid labor made possible the creation in the North of the American industrial cornucopia—and also from the deaths of the many millions of Native Americans who once walked and slept and cooked and thought on the very spots where US citizens now go to buy espresso machines, or reenact battles, or ski.

Obviously, no one can prove that a just world in which no one was subjugated and no one was oppressed would be a peaceful world in which no one would be tempted to murder his neighbor, and in which cruel practices and cruel ideologies would simply disappear, and the human race would reverse course and begin to devote itself to protecting the planet and all living creatures. But clearly if we simply keep going the way we're going now, a horrible death, for the rich as well as for the poor, surely can't be escaped. We need to find a path to a better world. Our only hope is to find that path.

We need a better world right away, this week. An upheaval is desirable—perhaps it's inevitable. And yet we've learned some things about ourselves over the last hundred years, and that knowledge makes a difference. We can't ignore the things we've learned. If, as a species, we start to find our way, through effort and imagination, toward a different sort of world, certain individuals and groups will find themselves taking the first steps, and one has to hope that they will keep what we've learned very much in mind. And the most important thing we've learned is that we don't understand ourselves.

We have to remember the murderer in the courtroom who said, "I don't know." We have to recognize that no matter who we are, even if we happen to be people who can honestly claim to have spent our whole lives struggling to create a better and more just world, all the same, we are human beings, and we don't know ourselves. We don't understand ourselves. But we do know for sure that other people and all living things need to be protected from us, because we're very dangerous. We may be unknowable, and it would be insane to trust us.

Even if what we want is a better life for everyone, we have to remember what species we belong to, and we have to watch ourselves very, very carefully.

Taking pleasure in triumphing over others, taking pleasure in having control over others, taking pleasure in telling others what to do, taking pleasure in the suffering of others, taking pleasure in being the cause of the suffering of others, taking pleasure in the death of others, and then, the extra thirty-seven blows that words can't seem to explain—what response can we have when this creature approaches?

Self-deception, too, we've learned, is a thunderingly powerful force in human affairs. No one can hide from it. No one is exempt from it. The ability to believe, falsely, that we know our own motives and that those motives are good, is an affliction that can befall those whose motives were once indeed good just as easily as it can befall those whose motives have always been bad. And just as the possession of wealth or a high status in society makes a person's engine of self-deception race faster, so too does the possession of power over others, and so too does the use of physical violence.

It seems undeniable that once it begins, violence leads us into some sort of madness, some terrifying maze inside the mind in which we become lost, and we don't know what's happening or what we ourselves are doing. In 1945, a group of us dropped an atomic bomb on the city of Hiroshima. Various people gave explanations for that. And then three days later, we dropped another atomic bomb on Nagasaki. Were there explanations for that as well? It doesn't matter. It really doesn't matter. I'm saying that the means of violence should not be entrusted to members of the human race. Power over the lives of other human beings should not be entrusted to members of the human race. I think that the long scientific experiment has given us some very clear results by now: humans are not equipped to handle these things.

Most of those who have dreamed of a more just world, who have perhaps spent their lives trying to prepare for one, have confronted the cold intransigence of the world's entrenched elites, the dug-in repositories of luck and strength, and they've come to the conclusion that these ruthlessly greedy and heartless people will never give up power if blood is not spilled, that only violence can possibly dislodge them. And yet those who triumph in violent combat are by definition triumphant; they're by definition victors, and they're by definition powerful, and, whatever else they are, at that moment of victory they're strong, and they're lucky. At least at that moment, they've become the lucky elite.

And this brings us naturally to the questions of revenge and punishment. Because if the unlucky were ever indeed to remove the lucky from their current position of supremacy, the issue of "what to do about the lucky" would immediately be on the table, and the questions of revenge and punishment would immediately arise.

We all, naturally, dream of revenge. It's one of the most enjoyable and thrilling of fantasies. We all become excited when we imagine the day when those whom we've learned to despise, those whom we feel have gotten away with so much for so long, will finally pay a price, will finally receive the reward they've earned. And yet—the person who takes revenge, at that very moment, becomes too powerful; the person who punishes, at that very moment, becomes too powerful.

Revenge and punishment both imply, "Even if I'd been you, and I'd had your life, I would never have done what you did." And that in turn implies, "I wouldn't have done it, because I'm better than you." But the person who says, "I'm better than you" is taking a serious step in a very dangerous direction. And the person who says, "Even if I'd had your life, I would never have done what you did" is very probably wrong.

There is a thing inside each of us that we experience as the will, the "I." We're all aware that there are warring impulses inside us, and sometimes we feel that our will is on one side and some powerful internal force is on the other side. Some people struggle not to drink alcohol. There's an institute in Sweden that helps principled people who find themselves struggling with a sexual attraction to children. In privileged societies, many people struggle with themselves not to eat the extra rolls that remain sitting on the table when the dinner is over. We all go through various sorts of struggles, and sometimes the thing we experience as our "I" wins, and sometimes it loses. What we don't know, though, and what science can't tell us, is whether it was ever possible for that struggle to have had a different outcome from the one it had. In my opinion, and I can't prove that I'm right, though I can't be proved wrong, the answer is probably never yes.

If two people compete in a game of tennis, no one knows who will win before the game begins. But when the game is over, it's often possible for a skilled observer to explain why the winner won. The outcome was ultimately determined by the way that the strengths and the weaknesses of the two players interacted in that particular game on that particular day in that particular place. Struggles that take place inside a human being are harder to observe, but I've never seen any reason to doubt that the facts about a person's current circumstances, in addition to the facts about their current personal makeup—their original genetically determined nature, changed and developed by the habits and beliefs and psychological characteristics they've acquired during their lives—determine the outcome of their inner struggles. The struggle inside the human being is real, just as the tennis game is real. Before the tennis game begins, no one knows what factors will influence it. No one knows, for example, that a sudden noise will distract one of the players at a crucial moment. All the same, the sum of the factors—including the sudden noise—will determine the outcome of the game. And in a similar way, the balance of forces within the individual—including their reactions to the environment around them—will determine the outcome of their inner struggles. If an alcoholic tries not to drink and fails, it's because their impulse to drink was too strong, or their will was too weak, or both were true, and in any case, their "I" "lost control" over their actions—that is, they did what their "I" truly didn't want to do. Did they struggle as hard as they could? We can't know whether they did or not. Did they create their own nature and determine how strong their will would be? No, they didn't.

I can decide that I want to become a better person. I can try to become a better person, and maybe I'll succeed. But I don't have the ability to discard all the elements of myself that may make that task of becoming a better person difficult.

When danger suddenly appears in our lives, and we need to make a choice—allow the escaped slave, hunted Jew, or undocumented refugee to hide in our house or send them away—we might turn out to be courageous, or we might turn out to be cowardly. In that moment of crisis, a vast number of factors that are hidden from our own consciousness are set feverishly to work inside us. Our fear of the price we might have to pay for a courageous choice is a factor, but so are the things our various friends and loved ones have said to us over the years, so are the books we may have read, so are the examples set by people we know and people we don't know. In the first moment of crisis, we have no idea what we're going to do. But to tell our friends today that if a crisis comes tomorrow, we know we'll be courageous, is simply foolish. And to righteously denounce the person who ultimately made the cowardly choice is foolish also. "Morality" may—if we're fortunate—tell us what the better choice is and help us to fight for it within ourselves. Morality can influence our behavior; perhaps in some cases it will determine our behavior. But the actual process of decision-making takes place in secrecy; it happens in a private room from which we're escorted out at the last moment. And even if we know what the right choice is, and we long to make that choice, the balance of forces inside us may compel us to go in the opposite direction.

Bernard Madoff was an intelligent and successful New York business executive who swindled a great many people out of an extraordinary amount of money. Radovan Karadžić was a Bosnian Serb psychiatrist, politician, and military commander who committed many war crimes during the 1990s Bosnian war, including ordering the deaths of eight thousand people in and around the town of Srebrenica, which the United Nations had declared to be a safe zone. Did Madoff have the ability not to swindle his clients? Did Karadžić have the ability not to massacre the people in Srebrenica? And what about me? If I'd been in their circumstances, would I have done the things they did? Possibly not, if I were still me. But if I had had Madoff's brain and Madoff's life, I would have been Madoff, and I think I would have done what Madoff did, and if I'd had Karadžić's brain and had had Karadžić's life, I would have been Karadžić, and I think I would have done what Karadžić did. And consequently I can't help feeling that the whole apparatus of blame, judging, hatred toward those who've done terrible things, is fundamentally wrong and ought to be discarded, and that punishment and revenge are based on assumptions that are fundamentally false.

Punishment is one of the possible techniques a community can use (a time-honored one, obviously) to indicate or emphasize what sort of behavior it doesn't like or doesn't condone, and the fear of punishment can certainly influence people's behavior. And in certain cases perhaps people find it actually enjoyable to exact revenge. All the same, punishment and revenge are both still unjust, because there's absolutely no way to determine that the person being punished, or the person against whom revenge is taken, was capable of behaving differently from the way they behaved.

Through no fault of their own, most unlucky people are born into bad circumstances from which no amount of ingenuity will allow them to escape. But also through no fault of their own, most lucky people are born into good circumstances, from which they may or may not want to escape but from which in any case they rarely do escape. Most of these lucky people lack the originality or the boldness or the imagination that would be required in order for them to give up their pleasant life and devote themselves to the welfare of humanity. And most are never provided with the intellectual tools they would need in order to see through the worship of greed and the self that the influential figures in their privileged environment are eager to teach them, and so they become greedy and selfish people. So let's try not to be hypocrites. Let's recognize that we all are born with a great number of capacities inside us, and then, well, life has its way with us. Certain of our capacities are activated, and others are not, and we turn out one way or another.

Some of us turn out to be brave, generous, and kind. Others turn out to be not particularly wonderful people. But there's no good reason to condemn, revile, punish, or kill the lucky, the privileged, or the greedy. If some of them are awful people, or if from a certain point of view they're all awful, they became awful through the same ordinary human process that applies to everybody.

We don't yet know how that human process works. What enables us to do good things or terrible things? Even among nations, the mechanism remains opaque. After World War Two, Germans quite rightly asked themselves, How could we have done what we did? They examined their culture, their child-raising practices, even their language, endlessly trying to comprehend, Why are we worse than other people? In the years since World War Two, though, it's been the jovial, friendly Americans, with a completely different culture, different child-raising practices, and a different language, who were responsible for ghastly activities in Vietnam, Latin America, Iraq, and a great many other places, while the Germans, retaining the same language they had before, along with much of the same culture and certain of the same child-raising practices, have kept themselves very low down on the list of postwar international killers. Casting one's mind back to days gone by, there are reasons to say that the Belgians are actually the worst people, but one could mention also the English, or the French. The honor of being the worst seems to travel strangely between nations, which means that each nation in itself is not intrinsically either demonic or not demonic, though, unsurprisingly, the Germans were horrifying in a German style, and the Americans are horrifying in an American style.

It's our desperate task to figure out what, exactly, activates this capacity for unspeakable behavior that we all possess. Those who hope to create a better world particularly need to brood about that question, because of the particular dangers they themselves might present if their struggle to change the existing order should manage to succeed. Success is dangerous. It's a lot like luck.

TEACHERS

The teachers in the fascinating schools I attended were subversively guiding us toward the "downward mobility" that some of us later experienced. They were quietly leading us away from our society's obsession with self, power, prestige, and money. Perhaps, they imagined, it might be possible for some of us, or all of us, to develop a character that was less grasping, more yielding. They were slyly giving us a hint that we might just possibly want to slip away altogether from the elite world of the lucky into which we'd been born. And I must have been listening to what those teachers were saying because not many years later I became deeply involved in a love affair with someone whose apartment was extremely small, with poorly installed plumbing—and whose feeling about the apartment was that it wasn't really that bad.

I myself still haven't escaped the desire for comfort. I like comfort, I like comfort enormously—even luxury, if I can get my hands on it. But my teachers softened me up, without any question. I'd say I'm halfway to decadence. My manliness gauge stands at more than half empty. And that's also true for many of my friends. And many of their friends. If someone says to me, "Your air conditioner uses energy sources that are raising the level of carbon dioxide in the atmosphere," I may take a hard look at the person who's saying it, think for a moment, and ignore what they said. But if all my friends gave up their air conditioning units, I wouldn't insist on keeping mine. And if some day next week or some day a few years from now, the great masses of the unlucky should come to my door and want to confiscate my air conditioner or even my entire apartment, I'm pretty sure that I won't fight them. I'm pretty sure I'll simply give up. I'll simply surrender. If some of my neighbors form an army of the lucky to fight the unlucky, I won't join. I'm much too lazy to fight for what I have, and what would make me an impossibly poor soldier in the army of the lucky is that I don't really believe I have a right to what I have. I know that my side is not the right side. I know that my life has always been wrong. So today I can easily live my life and enjoy my life, even love my life, but if the moment comes, I won't kill for it, and I won't even fight for it.

In other words, I'm saying that one way that a great upheaval could possibly occur without the shedding of blood would be if those who are now the lucky elite could already, today, be privately at work on quietly melting and softening their own shells, to use a snail metaphor, so that ultimately they would all become small worm-like creatures who wouldn't fight and couldn't fight. And this is not a preposterous fantasy. The children of the most ruthless executives and military leaders very often turn out to be delicate aesthetes who want nothing more than to play with puppets or make long necklaces out of small colored beads.

CIVILIZATION

The people who wrote the books with which Brecht quarreled didn't consider the possibility that civilization might have been a mistake. If they'd been asked about it, they probably would have agreed with the thin man who believed that Beethoven's music, being the end product of a process that saw humans go from hunting and gathering to being members of modern society, was a sort of infallible indicator that the process itself was purely admirable. If we confront Beethoven's music, they would probably have argued, we are confronting something that's undeniably good, and so the development of civilization, which led to Beethoven, can never be regretted. But this ignores the suffering that accompanied civilization. Because suffering is also a kind of absolute. When we see photographs of the fire in the sweatshop, when we see the pictures of the parents grieving over their daughters who worked in the sweatshop, we are face to face with what is undeniably not good.

If one were seriously to consider this odd question of the value of civilization, of course, one would need to speculate about the happiness or unhappiness of the hunter-gatherers who came before civilization—which is notoriously difficult to do—and one would need to guess whether the life of a hunter-gatherer in the Africa of many millennia ago was a better life than the life of a sweatshop worker in Africa today. And then, in brooding about the question of civilization, one would have to note that the worst consequences of civilization may not have occurred yet; they may be just around the corner. And one also has to note that we can't quite reach a verdict on civilization at the present moment, because it's at least theoretically possible that we might still be able to change course, to go in a different direction, and so we can't be sure that civilization won't eventually be twisted inside-out into a shape that will be enormously beneficial. In any case, civilization is what we have now, and so—short of a horrifying cataclysm—electricity, cities, books, poetry, mathematics, physics, paintings, and quartets will be the sorts of things we have at our disposal to work with if a better world is ever to be made.

To get from where we are now to some less terrifying place will be, if not completely impossible, certainly way beyond difficult, and so it almost goes without saying that the human beings who might carry out such an extraordinary creative task need to be as inspired and insightful and intelligent and deep as members of the species can possibly be. And here is where we must say that civilization itself could come in handy, because some of the things that civilization has learned how to do could prove remarkably useful in the struggle to save the world from some of the things that civilization is now doing. Because civilization has actually figured out how to store up and preserve human wisdom from over the millennia and has devised remarkable methods for refining and sharpening the individual human mind.

Civilization has come up with many precious objects that can cause the human mind to expand, but many of these objects have been hoarded in the locked treasure rooms of a tiny number of individuals. And many of the treasures have fallen victim to a fate that is common to things that are kept in locked rooms; no one quite remembers where they are, and after a while they're completely forgotten. We need to break into those rooms, because we need all the help we can possibly get.

There's no reason to doubt that every healthy human infant is born with the potential to play music beautifully, to read with sensitivity, to do scientific research, to put on plays, to draw and paint, and certainly to think. To think, to understand, to reason, to analyze arguments. And naturally also, to develop, to grow.

But almost all of those who are born unlucky have been brutally prevented from developing more than a fraction of their own abilities, and this is perhaps the most shocking fact about our human world.

Undoubtedly less shocking, but possibly more weird, is the incredible fact that in the contemporary world many even of those who are born lucky are voluntarily forgoing the opportunity to develop their inner resources. Gorgeous and delicious fruits, grown by seductive geniuses, sit on the plates of these lucky people but remain uneaten. A process of decay has infected the lucky in various lucky parts of the world, leading many even of the luckiest to turn vehemently against complex thought in general and the cultivation of the intellect in particular—and even to turn against complex pleasures. And in certain circles, crude thought and ignorance are openly respected and praised, while the concept of basing one's conclusions on demonstrable facts (or on replicable experiments)—and even the principle of rationality itself—is ignored or even mocked. Traveling in precisely the opposite of the direction that would help the world to dig itself out of its crisis, many lucky people have come to believe that our spiritual and mental lives should have only two elements: first, everyone should learn whatever technical skills are necessary in order for them to be able to work and make money (skills learned by the unlucky would bring them a small amount of money, skills learned by the lucky would bring them a large amount of money) and second, for relaxation, people should consume very simple pleasures such as very simple stories, very simple music, very simple eroticism, and various sadistic forms of amusement such as television programs that show people insulting or tormenting each other or killing each other. Omitted from this short list of recommended intellectual activities—and from the type of education that can be derived from it—is anything conducive to the development of the wide-awake, thoughtful, curious, sharply logical, and deeply emotional human beings who could save the world, on the one hand, or, if a better world were to be created, could actually enjoy it. And regrettably, the human beings whose mental life would conform to the plan these individuals consider desirable would be ill equipped intellectually to defend themselves against manipulation and control by cunning supporters of the status quo and all the glittering species of egomaniacs with whom we're all too familiar.

In other words, the expansion of every individual's potential would be what we would hope would happen in a better world, but if it doesn't happen to some extent in the world we're in now, we're never going to get to anything better.

THE LUCKY

If anyone is reading this, there may be members of the group of the lucky among them, and to them I would simply say, Yes, it is highly unlikely that a better world will come about, but if by some miracle it does, it may be better for you than you think it will be. Of course it will be difficult to break your habits and addictions, though, obviously, it will be somewhat easier for your children to break theirs. But if the time comes, you're going to be able to learn how to live without your car and your coffee-bean grinder. You could eventually get used to a life in which you didn't give orders. You could even get used to doing your share of the irreducible minimum of unpleasant labor that happens to be necessary to maintain the processes of life on which we all now depend. Vegetables must be grown in the countryside, and there are parts of the process of farming that can't be done by machines and that no one likes to do, and, in the cities, people have to crawl down under the streets to maintain the sewers, and in a more just world, the work that absolutely no one wants to do would probably have to be shared, with every able-bodied person doing some of it each week or each month, and so one of the people who'd be doing it would sometimes be you, and after a while you'd be quite all right with that. And yes, you'd have to live in a smaller apartment. Maybe a much, much smaller apartment, but if all went well, you'd still be able to read, cook, and play music, and after a while you might come to feel that it really wasn't that bad.

NIGHT

Night is a wonderful blessing. It's amazing, and I'm so grateful for it. In the darkness, lying in bed, we can stop. To be able to stop—that's amazing. We can stop. We can think. Of course it's frightening too. We think of what may happen to us. We think about death. Murders and murderers stand around the bed. But night gives us a chance to consider the possibility that we can start again, that when day comes we can begin again in a different way.

The aggressiveness that has been our daily mode of being can't help us any more. We wake up and start massacring people whom we see as our enemies. We wake up and break into the earth with gigantic drills and terrifying explosions. We wake up and find our place in a monstrous final struggle. On the one side, there are all the lucky people, and on the other side, strangely allied together, we find all the unlucky people, plus the birds, the crickets, the ladybugs, the bees, the monkeys, the parrots, the forests, and the rivers. At the moment, the lucky people are clearly winning, and almost all the evidence seems to indicate that they'll ultimately prevail. The nonhuman creatures and the unlucky people are running from place to place, gassed, strafed, shot at, booby-trapped, gasping for breath. And the living planet that we've blasted and bombed and injected with poison is now, like an enormous animal who's been tortured for hours by some horribly disturbed demented children, finally beginning to die, and its terrible groans are dreadful to hear. But the animal may not die, if we can convince the children, who are ourselves, to stop killing it. It's perhaps still a possibility that we might be able to stop being murderers. This could be our night, and during this night we might be able to stop. Stop. Think. And start again in a different way.

Acknowledgments for *Night Thoughts*

To publicly name the people who kindly offered thoughts on the manuscript of this essay might expose them to ridicule, so I won't do that, but I am enormously grateful to I, D, D, C, B, and A, you know who you are—and, *natürlich*, D.

A Note on the Text

Some of these pieces appeared previously in different places in a slightly different form. As they are now appearing between the covers of this book, and as I'm still alive, I haven't hesitated to fix things that seemed repetitious, illogical, mistaken, garbled, whatever.

—W.S. October, 2021

Sources

"Introduction to *Essays*": The book *Essays* was published in 2009 by Haymarket Books.

"After the Destruction of the World Trade Center" was originally published as "The Foreign Policy Therapist" in *The Nation*, December 3, 2001.

"The Quest for Superiority" was delivered as the Blashfield Foundation Address on May 21, 2008, at the Ceremonial of the American Academy of Arts and Letters in New York. It was originally published under the title "The Unobtrusives" in *Tin House.*

"Aesthetic Preferences" was originally published as "A Letter to the Reader" in *Our Late Night* and *A Thought in Three Parts: Two Plays*, Theatre Communications Group, 2008.

"Patriotism" was originally published in *The Nation*, July 15-22, 1991.

"Morality" was originally published as the Appendix to *Aunt Dan and Lemon*, Grove Weidenfeld, 1985.

"Interview with Mark Strand" was originally published as "Mark Strand: The Art of Poetry LXXVII" in The *Paris Review*, Fall, 1998.

"Breakfast Table with Jewish Newsletters" was originally published in the online edition of *The Nation*, January 1, 2021.

"Reading Plays" was originally published as the Author's Note in *Four Plays*, Noonday Press, Farrar, Straus and Giroux, 1997.

"Interview with Noam Chomsky" was originally published in *Final Edition*, autumn 2004.

"Myself and How I Got into Theatre" was originally published as the Introduction to *Plays One*, Faber and Faber, 1997.

"Writing About Sex" was originally published as the Afterword to *Our Late Night* and A *Thought in Three Parts: Two Plays*, Theatre Communications Group, 2008.

"Why I Call Myself A Socialist" began as a speech at the conference "Socialism 2010" in Chicago, Illinois, in June, 2010.

"Night Thoughts" began as a speech at the conference "Socialism 2016" in Chicago, Illinois, in July, 2016 and was subsequently published as a book by Haymarket Books in 2017.